W9-CCH-708

website owner's
manual

website owner's
manual

Paul Boag

MANNING

For online information and ordering of this and other Manning books, please visit www.manning.com. The publisher offers discounts on this book when ordered in quantity. For more information, please contact

Special Sales Department
Manning Publications Co.
Sound View Court 3B
fax: (609) 877-8256
Greenwich, CT 06830
Email: orders@manning.com

©2010 by Manning Publications Co. All rights reserved.

No part of this publication may be reproduced, stored in a retrieval system, or transmitted, in any form or by means electronic, mechanical, photocopying, or otherwise, without prior written permission of the publisher.

Many of the designations used by manufacturers and sellers to distinguish their products are claimed as trademarks. Where those designations appear in the book, and Manning Publications was aware of a trademark claim, the designations have been printed in initial caps or all caps.

Recognizing the importance of preserving what has been written, it is Manning's policy to have the books we publish printed on acid-free paper, and we exert our best efforts to that end. Recognizing also our responsibility to conserve the resources of our planet, Manning books are printed on paper that is at least 15 percent recycled and processed without the use of elemental chlorine.

Manning Publications Co.   Development Editor: Sebastian Stirling
Sound View Court 3B   Copyeditor: Tiffany Taylor
Greenwich, CT 06830   Designer: Leslie Haimes
                                  Illustrator: Eamon Dougherty

ISBN: 978-1-933988-45-0
© 2010
Printed in the United States of America
1 2 3 4 5 6 7 8 9 10 – MAL – 14 13 12 11 10 09

To my father, who inspired me to write a book;
and to my son, who may one day write one of his own.

CONTENTS

FOREWORD

In all of human history, there has never been a more exciting time to be alive than right now. I believe that we're on the cusp of a revolution that is more important and powerful than anything the world has ever seen.

Ubiquitous broadband, advanced browsers, cheap computing, and trust in online payments now allow us to launch our ideas cheaply, quickly, and effectively to a global audience.

On top of all that is the augmenting power of online social networks. We've witnessed the power of Facebook and Twitter to increase traffic to sites in unprecedented ways. These new tools are giving Google a run for its money in becoming the primary referral source for all websites. Who would've imagined?

The simple fact that you're reading this book means you're part of a very fortunate group of people who are uniquely placed to take advantage of this revolution. You're rich enough to own a computer. You're smart enough to understand HTML. You're lucky enough to be in your prime at this moment in history. If anyone has the opportunity to kick some serious ass and change the world, it's you.

The Internet is going to change the course of human history, and you'll be leading that charge. It's simply mind blowing.

Unfortunately, however, we still have a long way to go. It's hard to make an amazing website. For every great site, 99 other sites fail abysmally in their goals. There are a hundred different ways to fail with a website: poor copy, stale content, unintuitive user interfaces, bad color choices, lack of direction, inferior design, and more.

Wouldn't it be great if a straightforward manual was available for website owners? Guess what? You're holding it!

I'm glad that Paul has taken the time to compile his 10 years of experience in designing and building websites into this valuable book. It's the smartest money you've spent this year, and I guarantee you that it will revolutionize the way you approach your website.

See you in the history books!

RYAN CARSON
FOUNDER, CARSONIFIED.COM

PREFACE

Sometimes I feel like Bill Murray in the film *Groundhog Day*, doomed to endlessly repeat the same day. I find myself having the same conversations with website owners over and over again and encountering the same frustrating stories.

I've been designing websites since 1994 and have worked with hundreds of website owners. The majority of these clients share a similar story. They are marketers, project managers, business owners, and IT specialists who have for one reason or another found themselves responsible for their organization's website. They often have little or no experience with the web and so turn to an outside agency or freelancer for help.

Unfortunately, their experience of working with these contractors is often far from satisfactory. They're made to feel stupid, are overwhelmed with technobabble, and are asked to make significant decisions about their web strategy with next to no information. By the time I meet them, they're usually demoralized and cynical.

I wrote this book in an attempt to stop this cycle of failure. In many ways, it's a continuation of the work I've been doing for some time.

I enable website owners to take control of their sites. I do this by helping them understand their role, the key ingredients of a successful website, and how to work effectively with web designers.

Initially, I did this solely on a one-to-one basis. As clients came to work with my web-design agency (Headscape), I attempted to guide them through the process, educating them on the way. But it didn't take me long to realize that this approach had a limited reach.

In an attempt to reach a wider audience, I began blogging and podcasting on the subject. I quickly discovered that website owners weren't the only people interested in my ideas. Web designers also started to listen to my show and read my blog. They were keen to help their clients gain a better understanding of running a successful website. As interest in the blog and podcast grew, it led to speaking engagements and finally to this book.

For me, this book is the culmination of my attempt to better equip website owners. It brings together my own thoughts and the advice of others much cleverer than myself.

ACKNOWLEDGMENTS

I never considered writing a book or thought I'd have the opportunity to do so. It has been possible only because of support from many people. As you can imagine, I'm keen to thank them.

I'd like to particularly thank my father, who has always been my role model and inspiration. A talented wildlife photographer and author, he has written a number of books despite the fact that he failed English at school. His example made me realize that I was capable of writing a book, too. This belief was reinforced by the endless love and support of my mother, who, defying all logic and reason, believed me capable of anything.

Of course, just because I had the ability to write a book didn't mean I had the opportunity. Thanks for that opportunity belongs both to Manning for agreeing to take on this book and to my co-founders of Headscape, Marcus Lillington and Chris Scott. To all concerned, I apologize that the writing of this book took so much longer than expected!

In many ways, this book has been a group effort born out of years of discussion and debate with the Boagworld community. Without the input of these talented designers, developers, and website owners, this book would be much reduced. Although this community's members are too numerous to mention individually, I'd like to thank Ryan Taylor, Anna Debenham, and Paul Stanton, who have helped keep the site and podcast going when I was distracted by writing.

I also appreciate the help of Patrick Lauke, who was kind enough to be my technical editor. Without his scrutiny, I would have shown my ignorance on a number of occasions.

Special thanks to Ryan Carson for writing the foreword and to the following reviewers who read the manuscript at various stages in its development and provided valuable feedback: Aleksey Nudelman, Andy Yeates, Matthew Curry, Vincent Stoneking, Robert Hanson, Rob Allen, Sheldon Kotyk, Andrew Grothe, Robert Wenner, Gary Marshall, Chris Kelly, Radhakrishna M.V., Amos Bannister, Muhammad Saleem, Scott Stanlick, and Curt Christianson.

Finally, I could not end without thanking Catherine, my wife. She is my world, and I love her more than life itself. Without a doubt, this book would never have been written if it wasn't for her love, support, and most of all patience.

ABOUT THIS BOOK

Welcome to the *Website Owner's Manual*! If you've picked up this book, you probably run a website and want advice about how to make it more successful.

There is certainly no shortage of advice available, in the form of books, conferences, blogs, podcasts, magazines, and tutorials. These offer an unbelievable amount of detail; for example, entire books dedicated to designing website forms and blogs only look at online typography. The problem is not too little advice but too much!

Even if you had endless time to review all this information, with so many sources and such depth available, it's impossible to know where to begin. This book endeavors to overcome this problem.

The *Website Owner's Manual* provides an overview of running a successful website. It focuses on the issues you need to know and teaches you how to work with experts for everything else.

It covers your own role as website owner and looks at strategic issues such as business objectives, target audiences, and success criteria. It goes on to teach you how to work with web designers, content providers, and technical developers. It also provides a basic understanding of design, usability, best practices, content creation, and online marketing.

In short, it is a manual for website owners.

Who should read this book?

As the title suggests, this book is primarily for website owners. But who are website owners? Chances are you don't describe yourself as one, but this book is probably still for you.

A *website owner* is anyone who is responsible for their organization's website. That doesn't mean you have to be a web expert. There are few full-time, highly qualified website owners. Most are marketers, project managers, IT professionals, or business owners who have either been given the job of running a website or have volunteered because nobody else would.

Often, the website is just one more responsibility alongside your official job description. Most website owners lack any training in the role and have little experience managing websites.

If that sounds like you, then this book is the answer. I wrote it to tell you all you need to know about running a successful website.

But this book also has a lot to offer web professionals. If you're an experienced website manager, this book will serve as a useful checklist when you're initiating new projects and will bring you up to date with current best practices.

If you're a web designer or developer working with clients or management, this book will provide you with valuable insights into effective communication and how to guide a client through the process of building a website.

Roadmap

Website Owner's Manual guides you through the various stages of planning, building, and running a website. The principles laid out in this book apply whether you're building a website for the first time, relaunching an existing site, or adding functionality.

Each chapter deals with a different aspect of web design:

> **Chapter 1** defines the role of a website owner. It explains that this role is the key to a successful website and examines some the challenges involved.

> **Chapter 2** addresses the importance of planning. In particular, it tackles understanding your users, learning from the competition, and analyzing your existing site. It also asks, "How will you judge your project a success?"

> **Chapter 3** focuses on recruiting the team you need to build your website and ensuring that you clearly communicate with that team.

> **Chapter 4** looks at the contentious issue of design. It provides advice about working with a designer and how to select a final design less subjectively. It also explains some basic design principles and tackles the thorny subject of the home page.

> **Chapter 5** deals with the biggest challenge facing most website owners: content. It looks at writing user-friendly content, organizing that content, and understanding the importance of context.

> **Chapter 6** is about making your site more user friendly. It presents a business case for usability testing and tells you how to test your own site at minimal expense.

> **Chapter 7** goes on to address best practices in web design. These include accessibility for both users and search engines, as well as the need to separate content from design.

> **Chapter 8** tells you all you need to know about selecting a content-management system. It also offers a word of warning about seeing such systems as silver bullets.

> **Chapter 9** explains the fundamentals about how the web works and helps decode the technobabble used by many web designers.

> **Chapter 10** looks at driving traffic to your website through the use of search engines and other marketing methods. It goes on to demonstrate how you can monitor these strategies.

> **Chapter 11** explains how a successful website facilitates a conversation between users and the site owner. It suggests practical ways to engage with users and nurture community.

> **Chapter 12** concludes the book by looking to the future. It stresses the need for continual development and focuses on emerging trends.

AUTHOR ONLINE

The purchase of the *Website Owners Manual* includes free access to a private forum run by Manning Publications where you can make comments about the book, ask technical questions, and receive help from the authors and other users. You can access and subscribe to the forum at http://www.manning.com/WebsiteOwnersManual. This page provides information about how to get on the forum after you register, the kind of help that's available, and the rules of conduct in the forum.

Manning's commitment to readers is to provide a venue where a meaningful dialogue between individual readers and between readers and the author can take place. It isn't a commitment to any specific amount of participation on the part of the author, whose contributions to the book's forum remain voluntary (and unpaid). We suggest you try asking the author some challenging questions, lest his interest stray!

The Author Online forum and the archives of previous discussions will be accessible from the publisher's website as long as the book is in print.

In addition to the Author Online forum available on Manning's website, you may also wish to visit the author's personal site at http://boagworld.com. From here, you can

> ➤ Access a wealth of additional articles about running a successful website.

> ➤ Participate in a vibrant community made up of designers, developers, and website owners.

> ➤ Subscribe to the author's award-winning podcast, which provides valuable insights into running a website.

> ➤ Follow the author's hints and tips on website management through social networks such as Twitter.

The site is designed to keep any website owner up to date with the latest innovations and best practices.

ABOUT THE AUTHOR

Paul Boag is a website strategist and a director at Headscape, a web-design agency based in the south of England. He started designing websites while working for IBM back in 1994. This was in the days when designing for the web was considerably easier. Since then, he has ridden the dot-com bubble and co-founded his own web-design agency.

Today, he can be found advising clients on how to better utilize the web, speaking around the world, and hosting the award-winning Boagworld web-design podcast. He also writes for his own blog and numerous other publications.

At the time of writing, he is addicted to Twitter. It will pass.

1

The secret to a successful website

In this chapter

Here's the million-dollar question:

"What is the secret to a successful website?"

I'm not foolish enough to suggest a single answer. But in my decade of working on client websites, I've noticed a recurring pattern: the sites that succeed are those that have a well-informed, passionate website owner at the helm. No single thing makes a site successful, but a good website owner puts into place the elements that give a site a fighting chance.

The question should be not "What is the secret to a successful website?" but "How do I become a great website owner?"

No definitive manual exists that explains how to do the job.

What does it mean to be a website owner, and how can you do it successfully?

DISCOVER YOUR MISSING MANUAL

The lack of a manual defining the role of website owner is only part of the problem. There is also a lack of training specific to being a website owner. Courses are available for web designers and developers, so it seems natural that website owners will be next. Meanwhile, this book endeavors to be your missing manual.

This book isn't the only available resource on being a website owner. Knowing how to handle the plethora of information available both in print and on the web is crucial to succeeding in your role.

Battling information overload

When it comes to learning how to run a successful website, the problem of information overload is particularly acute. Millions of web pages are dedicated to every conceivable aspect of website management, from usability testing to search-engine placement.

The offline world is no better. Hundreds of books cover the various facets of web design. Add to these conferences, magazines, seminars, and workshops, and it become impossible to identify what you need to know.

The problem is made worse because sources can often be out of date due to the rapid development of the web. This leaves you confused about current best practice. With so many evolving and often conflicting sources, how can you begin to know what is important?

Seeing the bigger picture

A good starting point is to recognize that a website owner is a generalist rather than a specialist. Think of yourself as a family doctor rather than a brain surgeon.

Family doctors deal with a huge variety of illnesses, from the common cold to complex

With so much information available from books, websites, magazines, conferences, and even podcasts, there is simply too much to learn.

If you focus on the wrong thing, it's easier to miss the larger picture. Maintain a broad overview, and let experts deal with specifics.

neurological problems. But they don't necessarily treat every illness they see. In the same way, a good website owner has enough knowledge to identify an issue and recognize that a specialist is required to deal with it.

In short, you should focus on the big picture of web design and know enough to manage the specialists who are occasionally required.

Having a "need to know" mentality

Good website owners should be able to identify what they "needs to know" rather than try to understand every aspect of the whole. Becoming a great website owner isn't just about understanding a web technology or knowing specific pieces of information. It's about grasping the role and approaching it with a certain mentality.

Three principles of website management encapsulate this mentality:

> Balancing conflicting priorities

> Defining your role

> Planning for the future

The most important of these principles is the need to maintain a balance between conflicting priorities.

PRINCIPLE 1. BALANCE CONFLICTING PRIORITIES

Balancing the various conflicting priorities in web design is like constructing a building. A building is made up of a series of pillars. If one pillar is shorter than the others or missing entirely, then the building is in danger of collapsing.

As in construction, it's vital that the pillars of web design have equal priority and that you ensure a balance among them all. The six pillars of web design are shown on the next page.

Making your site easy to use

Difficult sites can alienate visitors, causing them to give up. Later, we'll investigate ways to make your site more usable through card sorting and user testing.

For now, it's important to stress that as with any pillar, too much emphasis on usability can be damaging. If you're obsessed with usability, you can undermine business objectives, fail to engage with users emotionally (through aesthetics), and even create accessibility problems.

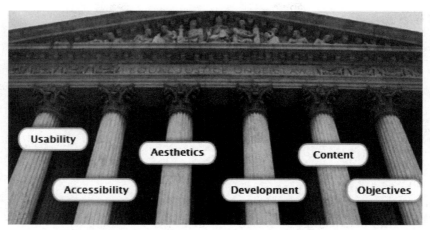

Every site is built using six disciplines that are vital to its success.

Providing access for all

Accessibility is easy to ignore as a marginal concern. But there are many good reasons to emphasize it: commercial incentives, legal commitments, and moral obligations.

Many website owners reject accessibility because they believe it's too expensive, it's difficult to implement, or it will negatively affect the site's aesthetics. But it's possible for good accessibility to exist comfortably alongside the next pillar.

More information

Many of the pillars of web design are covered in more depth later in this book. For more information, see the following chapters:

- Chapter 2: Objectives
- Chapter 4: Aesthetics
- Chapter 5: Content
- Chapter 6: Usability
- Chapter 7: Accessibility
- Chapter 9: Development

Producing aesthetic appeal

Aesthetics refer to the elements that make up the look and feel of your site. These include color, imagery, typography, and layout. Historically, website owners viewed aesthetics as the most important pillar of web design. This bias toward aesthetics was prevalent in the late 1990s and early 2000s and led to the proliferation of splash screens and a gratuitous use of Flash.

A heavy bias toward aesthetics damages not only usability but also most of the other pillars of web design. Fortunately, we're beginning to see less emphasis on design to the exclusion of the other pillars. We're also seeing a closer working relationship with the other pillars, especially development.

Facilitating development

Development refers to the technical aspects of a project. Many website owners find this pillar intimidating and so choose to ignore it. They want the functionality but aren't necessarily concerned with how it's delivered.

Although you can't be expected to understand the complexities of technical development, it's dangerous to ignore the constraints and challenges faced by technical developers. Technical development is evolving at a staggering rate, and if you don't engage with technical specialists, you'll miss opportunities to enhance your site.

aceofcakestv.com used to be so concerned with aesthetics that it was impossible to access without the Flash plug-in. Even if you had the plug-in, the site was incredibly difficult to navigate.

Of course, technical development can't be left to grow unchecked. As some sites built entirely by techies show, unfettered technical development can damage usability, accessibility, aesthetics, and, of course, content.

Creating killer content

Although content creation is one of the website owner's principle roles, it's often neglected. Perhaps this is because it isn't as sexy as aesthetics—or because creating content is hard work. It's easier to copy and paste content from an existing brochure or out-of-date website than it is to write content from scratch. Of course, some website owners are reluctant to write content because they have no experience in writing web copy, let alone any training. This is why an increasing number of website owners are employing experienced copy editors.

One of the problems faced by website owners is being able to interpret the seemingly foreign language spoken by many developers. In chapter 9, we'll explore some of this technobabble and discuss ways of improving communication.

Focusing on objectives

A site's objectives should occupy most of your attention as the website owner. Objectives refer to the business rationale behind a site. Why does it exist? What is it trying to achieve? How is success measured?

You could argue that objectives aren't a pillar. You write good copy, design an attractive site, and make it usable in an attempt to fulfill your site objectives. Site objectives are the target you're trying to reach, not the method by which you reach it. But I've found that thinking of objectives alongside usability, accessibility, aesthetics, and the rest creates a more rounded approach that should be encouraged.

The aim is to create a balance among all six pillars. If you can achieve this, you have built a good foundation upon which to construct a successful site.

Your site objectives are the goal that the other areas of web design allow you to reach.

The dangers of focusing on objectives in isolation

I once worked with a client whose objective was to generate sales leads. They became obsessed with that objective. They insisted that a user must register before they were allowed to view their product. Each registrant then became a sales lead. Although the client saw a slight increase in leads, ultimately they damaged their business.

Users actively wanted to view the client's product, but the barrier to entry was enough to drive them away. These visitors never matured into quality sales leads. Although some users did complete the form, most were not ready for a sales call. They only registered to access the demo, and so the quality of the leads was low. The work involved in following up these leads put a greater burden on the sales team without generating more sales.

By considering user needs, not just site objectives, my client might have produced fewer leads, but the quality of those leads would have been higher.

PRINCIPLE 2. DEFINE YOUR ROLE

The second principle of good website management is to have a clear vision for your role. Being a website owner is one of the most multifaceted jobs in the web development process. Because of this diversity, the role is often poorly defined. Failing to give the role boundaries can create two problems:

> *A lack of definition leads to a lack of focus.* Without a job description, you can find yourself drawn into unrelated work. Worse still, others can presume something is your responsibility when it isn't.

> *A lack of definition causes anxiety.* There is always a vague feeling that you aren't fulfilling your role or are perceived that way. By defining the role clearly, you allay your fears and establish others' expectations.

I recommend defining broad principles of responsibility, against which you can measure specific tasks. Here are six roles a good website owner should fulfill:

> Visionary   > Content guardian

> Advocate   > Project coordinator

> Evangelist   > Referee

Let's look at each of these roles in turn.

It's important to define the role of site owner and provide
the time and resources to fulfill it.

Having a vision

A good website owner should have a clear vision and be capable of developing it over the long term. This vision will evolve through discussions among the site's stakeholders.

When a site is being developed with the assistance of a web-design agency, it's good practice to include them in shaping the vision. Unfortunately, web-design agencies are often brought on board after the vision has been formed, so their input is missed. This can cause problems further down the line, as we'll cover in more detail later.

You need to have a clear picture of what role the site plays within your organization and how that role could be expanded later. The vision for your site should fall into two categories: the core vision and the roadmap.

Establish your vision

First is the *core vision*, which is the unshakable objective for the site. Consider a website that sells luxury vacations. The user's objective may be to "make planning and booking the customer's dream vacation a pleasurable and intuitive experience, thus increasing online sales."

This core vision for the site is unlikely to change over time and acts as a measure against which site developments can be compared. Each time the site considers a new piece of functionality, they can ask themselves, "Will this modification increase sales by making planning and booking easier and more pleasurable?"

Know your roadmap

The second category is the *roadmap*. This is a vision of how your site will develop over the coming months and even years. What kind of new functionality are you planning to add, and how is the user base expected to change?

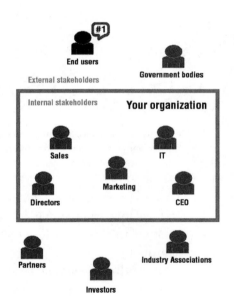

Who are your stakeholders?
Stakeholders are the people and organizations both internally and externally who have some interest in your site. The most important stakeholder should always be the end user.

In the case of our example, roadmap items may include adding an itinerary planner or allowing email subscriptions to receive the latest offers. It can include details on how to cater to a new market or support upcoming marketing campaigns.

Without a good understanding of the overall vision and roadmap ahead, a site can easily wander off track and lose its focus.

Being an advocate

The website owner should defend the site against varying agendas from different departments within an organization.

Establishing a vision is one thing; maintaining it is another. The vision needs an advocate: somebody willing to defend the site against others within the organization who might seek to undermine its focus.

The problem is particularly acute in larger organizations where people have a departmental rather than corporate perspective. This outlook leads to sites falling victim to internal politics and to individual departments pushing their own agendas.

Earlier in this chapter, I mentioned a website where users were forced to register before viewing a product demonstration. The problem arose because nobody was defending the vision to generate high-quality sales opportunities. Instead, the marketing department ran the show, and their agenda overruled the site's vision. They didn't care about the quality of the leads because that was "sales' problem." All they cared about was meeting their quota.

Although this example is an extreme case, I've seen similar things happen when departments fight over home-page space and top-level navigation. It falls to you to keep in mind the bigger picture and avoid this kind of provincial thinking.

Evangelizing your site

The danger of being a site's advocate is that you're on the defensive, constantly battling internal stakeholders. This can lead to the site becoming isolated from the rest of your organization and therefore adding little value.

It's important that your role be not just defensive but offensive too. Continually seek out ways the website can support operations within the company by maintaining a dialogue with the various departments and individuals.

A good website owner seeks to understand the challenges faced by others in the company and look for ways that the website can help with those issues. You can also evangelize the benefits of the web and keep your colleagues informed about the latest innovations that may apply to their situation.

Managing your content

Although roles such as visionary, advocate, and evangelist are important, they can be conceptual in nature. The more practical, demanding, and time-consuming role is your responsibility for the content of the site. This falls into three categories:

By talking to other departmental heads, you can quickly identify areas where the website can help meet organizational objectives.

> Populating initial content

> Keeping content fresh

> Ensuring a consistent message

Populating initial content

Content responsibility is the most time-consuming aspect of a website owner's role, and content population in the initial build phase is the most demanding element of that aspect. Writing and collating content for a website is a huge undertaking and the biggest reason that web projects fall behind schedule.

It's easy to underestimate the time involved in pulling together content from different sources and repurposing it in a format suitable for the web.

Keeping content fresh

Even after the initial site has been launched, your responsibility toward content doesn't end. You also need to keep the content fresh and up to date.

A website owner needs to continually source new content, review existing copy, and update as necessary. You need new content, such as news stories, to keep users coming back for more.

Ensuring a consistent message and tone

The job of generating content can become too big for a single person. You may choose to solve this problem by reusing existing content or turning to others for help. These approaches are perfectly valid. But they present the danger of inconsistency in both tone and content. You must ensure that the site speaks with a single unified voice.

You need to review each new piece of content added to your site. Does it use the same tone of voice used elsewhere on the site? Is the writing style the same? Are the facts quoted in line with what is already being shown?

In chapter 5, "Creating killer content," we'll talk more about generating content; for now, all you need is a clear picture of the owner's role in the process. That role involves coordinating, generating, and standardizing content.

Without a website owner ensuring consistent tone, a website can appear to have a split personality, with different sections written in different ways.

Coordinating your projects

Content contributors aren't the only people who need managing in a web design project. There are designers, developers, usability experts, hosting companies, and many more.

Although frequently you'll turn to a web-design agency to handle the management of these roles, it's inevitable that some management will be required internally. For example, internal sign-off is often required for project components such as budget, design, and content.

Unfortunately, the final role that most website owners have to fulfill is unofficial referee.

Resolving disagreements

Running a website is all about compromise. Compromises are necessary regarding content and which sections of the organization get the highest priority. You must compromise between the different pillars of web design and compromise about budget and time scales.

It is your job as website owner to resolve disagreements over priorities.

The various stakeholders have different perspectives on what is important. It's your responsibility to break any stalemates that occur by finding the middle ground. You have to be the decision maker.

Recognizing your role is an important step in being a great website owner, but it isn't the end of the journey. It's also important to realize that the role is ongoing and that the work of a website owner is never done.

PRINCIPLE 3. PLAN FOR THE FUTURE

Many organizations underestimate the enormity of the job faced by website owners, because they fail to grasp that it's a long-term commitment. This explains why so few organizations have full-time website owners despite the fact that they consider their website an important asset. A website owner is needed through the entire life cycle of a website to ensure that it evolves and remains successful.

Evaluating your objectives

You should constantly evaluate the website's objectives and ask if its overall vision and direction need changing. This doesn't have to happen on a daily basis but should be done every few months.

When reviewing your site, it's important to consider questions such as these:

> Have the underlying objectives of the website changed?

> How is the site performing against its success criteria, and are they still relevant?

> What is the competition doing, and how are you performing against them?

> How has the target audience changed, and what do they say about your site?

Website management is a cycle of planning, building, and growing your site. You should be constantly evaluating, and making changes based on what you learn to keep your site fresh.

In the next chapter, we'll look in detail at this subject. For now, remember that your objectives need to be reviewed regularly and that you should refine the site based on changes that arise.

Constantly evaluate your site, looking for ways the design, content, or functionality can be improved.

Refining your website

Responding to changes in site objectives can manifest itself in various forms. For example, if the success criteria for the site aren't being met, then you need to address that issue. Equally, if the competition is luring away your visitors, then the site needs to be altered to encourage them back. This continual tweaking of your site happens in three ways:

> Changes to the design

> The introduction of new functionality

> The addition, deletion, and editing of content

For example, the luxury vacation service I mentioned earlier might respond to increased competition by adding a flight price-comparison tool (new functionality). This would appeal to users and would draw them away from the competition. Alternatively, the site might add reviews of existing destinations (new content) to encourage repeat visitors. Finally, they could refine the design based on user opinion to make it easier to navigate (changes to design).

Responding to user comments is often the best way to refine your website. In chapter 6, "User-centric design," we'll address how to gather user feedback and use it to inform the changes you make. But first, we need to address the last of a website owner's ongoing roles: site promotion.

Promoting your site

Budget is rarely assigned to employ a specialist in site promotion, so it often falls to the website owner to fulfill this role. The number of visitors coming to your website will decline if you don't actively and regularly promote it.

You can effectively promote your site many ways, including the following:

Promotion type	Description
Offline promotion	Offline promotion includes letterheads, business cards, signage, phone systems, and other marketing collateral.
Email marketing	Email can be a powerful marketing tool to drive new traffic and a good way of encouraging existing users to return to your site.
Search mechanisms	Search mechanisms involve more than good placement on Google. They also include pay-per-click campaigns and social networking tools.
Guerilla marketing	*Guerilla marketing* is a catchall term for low-cost marketing methods. It includes techniques like community participation, viral marketing, blogging, and even podcasting.

Later, we'll explore how you can begin to promote your site using these and other techniques. For now, it's important to understand that site promotion requires a regular commitment (either internal or external). You should decide from the outset who will be responsible for this work.

Next actions

This chapter has looked at the role of website owner and its associated responsibilities. I'd like to end by proposing three tangible actions you can take to embrace the role:

ACTION 1: *Formalize the role of website owner.* The best way to formalize this role is for it to be written into your job description. Your responsibilities should be clearly defined, and time should be allocated to the role. Go to your boss and discuss what is expected.

ACTION 2: *Set aside regular time.* Just because the role has theoretical time allocated to it doesn't mean your website will get the attention it deserves. Try to fence off a certain amount of time every week that will be dedicated to the website. Don't allow more pressing responsibilities to push that time out. This will allow you to review the progress of your site and ensure that it's updated and promoted.

ACTION 3: *Review and plan before proceeding.* Even if you believe you have a clear picture of what needs to be done on your website, set aside a block of time to review the current state of your online presence. With deadlines imminent and management keen to see results, it's tempting to focus on site building or promotion. Resist the temptation to rush in. Plan your next step.

Planning is crucial to the success of a website. It's where you clarify the background of your web project, define its objectives, and decide how its success will be measured. Planning give you the opportunity to assess the competition, review your existing site, and better understand your target audience. It shouldn't be a surprise that the next chapter addresses planning.

2

Stress-free planning

In this chapter

W hen it comes to self-assembly furniture, I'm a disaster. I'm so bad at putting it together that my wife Catherine has banned me from trying and now does it herself. I start out enthusiastic, but within a few minutes I'm swearing like a trooper and repeatedly hitting planks of wood with whatever implement is near.

Catherine, on the other hand, is always composed and in control. She plans what needs to be done. Before she begins, she carefully reads all the instructions and collects the tools she'll require.

In contrast, I believe instructions are for dummies and that I intuitively know where all the pieces fit. As a result, I take three times longer than my wife does and become infinitely more stressed.

As with assembling flat-pack furniture, if you plan your website development process up front, you'll have a considerably less stressful experience. What is more, the result will be better.

KEEP YOUR PLANNING LIGHTWEIGHT

We all know how important it is to plan a project, but knowing something and doing it are different things. I know I should think before assembling furniture, but I'm so keen to "get started" and "not waste time" that planning goes out the window.

Effective planning for a web project should be lightweight and flexible.

The same can be true of running a website. Saving time by shortcutting planning is a false economy. Before long, problems will arise; and without up-front planning, they will lead to slippages in the project. Unless a project is clearly defined from the outset, people will have very different expectations of the result and their own responsibilities. This inevitably leads to conflict and more stress for the website owner.

Planning is often perceived as time-consuming and heavyweight. When I talk about planning a web project, I mean a lightweight process focused on developing a clearly defined vision and ensuring that all stakeholders in the project are consulted. This approach can be applied equally to a single new piece of functionality or a major overhaul of your entire web presence. This lightweight approach consists of the following stages:

> Understanding the broader context of your project

> Deciding how to judge the success of your project

> Assessing the project against your existing site

> Comparing the project to the competition

> Ensuring that you understand the audience for the project

Let's begin by understanding the broader context of your project.

DON'T PLAN IN A BUBBLE

You can't develop a vision for your site in isolation. It must be developed within a broader context. But what is that broader context, and how do you understand it?

Understanding the context of your web project

Whether you're developing an entire site or a single piece of functionality, there is always a context. New functionality exists within the context of its parent site. The site itself exists within the broader context of your organization and its strategies. This forms three layers of context that you need to consider:

The Three Layers of Context

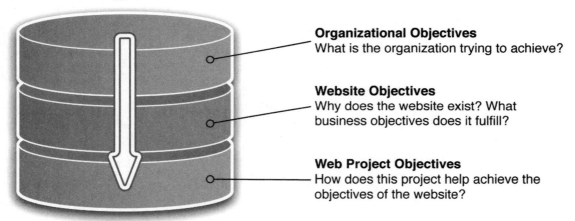

Organizational Objectives
What is the organization trying to achieve?

Website Objectives
Why does the website exist? What business objectives does it fulfill?

Web Project Objectives
How does this project help achieve the objectives of the website?

Each layer affects the one below with organizational context that relates to website objectives. This in turn influences individual web projects. Understanding each layer helps inform decisions you make regarding functionality and priorities in any individual project.

The detail you should collate largely depends on the complexity of the project and the time available for planning. In an ideal world, you would want to give significant thought to this broader context. But even the most basic consideration is better than none.

Let's look at a basic example of broader context by referring to our fictional vacation company, Dream Destination.

Dream Destination strategy

Like many businesses, Dream Destination has a strategy document that outlines the company's short- and long-term objectives. It also contains a mission statement. From this strategy document, the website owner learns that Dream Destination aims to "provide luxury, custom-designed dream vacations using its team of expert travel specialists." The company's current objective is to "break into the affluent over-60s market."

A real strategy document would say a lot more. But even this basic information helps the website owner define the role of the website. Look how key phrases from the strategy document can influence the website:

Quote from strategy	Consequences for website
" luxury... dream vacation"	The site design needs to convey a sense of quality and clearly distinguish itself from budget operators.
"Expert travel specialists"	The site shouldn't allow users to book directly. Instead, it should refer them to a specialist who will design a custom vacation itinerary.
"Affluent over 60s market"	This market has specific usability and accessibility requirements that will need to be accommodated.

You can promote a website in a number of different ways. This table gives you a basic outline of the key methods we'll explore in more depth later in this book.

The Dream Destination strategy document helps form a vision for the website. But it should also be informed by speaking with the site's stakeholders.

Gaining context through consultation

We established in chapter 1, "The secret to a successful website," that a *stakeholder* is anybody with a vested interest in the site. At Dream Destination, one set of stakeholders would be the "expert travel specialists."

Talking to stakeholders while planning a web project is an invaluable way of understanding the broader context of the project. Website owners sometimes dismiss stakeholders because they "don't know anything about the web." But the role of the website is to help these stakeholders achieve their business objectives. Their input will help shape the website's vision.

Take the "expert travel specialists." They deal with end users every day and can provide valuable insight into the target audience. They're also aware of problems that the website could fix. For example:

Stakeholder comment	Action generated
"Users give up because the inquiry form is too complicated."	Review the inquiry form, and look for ways to simplify the process by removing steps.
"We have to call the user with additional questions."	Make sure the inquiry form contains all the questions a specialist needs answered in order to provide a quote.
"Some of the inquiries seem to get lost."	Analyze what is causing inquiries to be lost, and develop an improved management system.

By repeating this process with other stakeholders across the organization, you can build up a picture of how the website can help achieve business objectives.

Spending time with your stakeholders also has a political benefit. A primary reason why web projects stall is objections from stakeholders. If the CEO or head of sales has a problem with the project, it can't progress. One reason they often object is because they aren't consulted during the project.

By speaking with stakeholders during the planning stage, you achieve two things. First, you identify any objections they may have up front, giving yourself an opportunity to tackle those objections before they become an issue. Second, you give the stakeholders the opportunity to express their concerns and requirements. This makes them feel engaged in the process. If somebody has been consulted, they're much less likely to object further down the line.

Running a series of stakeholder meetings is straightforward. Begin by arranging one-to-one meetings of between 45 minutes and an hour with each of your stakeholders. Be sure to leave some time between sessions in case somebody is particularly enthusiastic—it's important that a stakeholder cover all the subjects of concern to them.

What you cover in a session is largely dependent on how well you know the person and what role they have. Here are some suggestions:

Discussion point	Reason for including
"Tell me about your role and that of your department."	This request provides a context for the conversation. It helps you identify areas worth discussing in more depth.
"Talk to me about the processes you use in your average work day to get things done."	This builds up a picture of the stakeholders' working practices and identifies areas where the website could aid or hinder that process.
"What are the most time consuming and challenging parts of your job?	By asking about challenges, you may discover ways that web technologies can help overcome those challenges more efficiently.
"What company data or applications do you work with regularly in your job?"	Asking about data and applications can lead to valuable information and resources that can be used on the web.
"Tell me what you think of the company website and how you think it could be improved."	Getting the stakeholders' feedback on the website is invaluable and has obvious direct applications. It also makes the stakeholders feel that their opinions are valued.

Ultimately, the objective of a stakeholder interview is to identify areas where the website can aid stakeholders in fulfilling their role of meeting company objectives. After you've gathered background context and completed your stakeholder interviews, the next step is to distill your vision into measurable goals. These are called *success criteria*.

MEASURE SUCCESS

Having a vision provides context from which to build, but you also need a clearly defined set of success criteria. Success criteria provide three distinct benefits:

> *Measurable objectives*—Whereas the broad vision for a site talks about a desire to "boost sales" or "increase dwell time," success criteria set specific goals.

> *Justification for investment*—When you can't categorically state that your objectives have been met, it's hard to justify further investment. Success criteria provide that justification.

> *Improved communication*—I've witnessed projects where the developer's expectations were wildly different from management's. Discovering these differences at the end of a project leads to conflict. Working together to define realistic goals avoids recrimination later.

Although success criteria can be beneficial, they do carry risks.

Be specific in your goals

 "The website should significantly boost sales over the next few months"

 "The website should provide a 25% increase in online sales enquiries over the next 6 months"

Multiple criteria

Most web projects have multiple success criteria associated with them. If multiple goals are assigned, it's important that you prioritize them. When success criteria aren't prioritized, they end up conflicting and causing confusion rather than clarity.

Avoiding unrealistic goals

Setting success criteria should be a collaborative process among all those involved. Everybody should have a sense of ownership and be committed to achieving the agreed-on criteria.

The issue of unrealistic goals is more common than you might expect. The most common such goals are unrealistic time scales and budgets. Imposing these kinds of criteria without consultation can be a dangerous road, especially when you're

Goals should be agreed on by all parties, not imposed by management.

dealing with external agencies desperate to win your work and willing to say whatever it takes. Externally imposed success criteria inevitably lead to recriminations further down the line.

Avoiding the blame game

Assigning blame can be damaging to the morale of the web team. It's also unrealistic to attribute blame to any individual. Web projects are complex, with each person's contribution depending on many others. If you start blaming developers for late delivery, they're just as likely to blame you for a poorly defined scope of work. Nobody wins.

A better approach is to discuss, when the project is over, whether it fulfilled the success criteria. Usually, this can't happen immediately, because success criteria are fulfilled over time. When that meeting does take place, it should always look forward rather than focus on the past mistakes.

Consider why the project didn't meet expectations. Was it because the expectations were unrealistic? Did a problem arise that couldn't have been anticipated in advance? Ask these questions to ensure that these issues can be overcome in the future. For example, concluding that the success criteria were unrealistic enables you to revise them going forward. Identifying that a project was delayed due to unforeseen problems tells you to build in contingency plans next time.

You can also use this principle of looking back to plan for the future to analyze your existing site and help decide on future development.

Attributing blame for a failing website is ultimately counterproductive because no single individual is ever entirely responsible.

KNOW YOUR SITE

Start planning the future of your website by analyzing what you already have. A more formal approach helps to better inform your decision-making throughout the web project. Qualitative and quantitative feedback are two ways to better understand your current website.

To obtain qualitative feedback, you request comments from stakeholders and users. This type of feedback is traditionally gathered using the following techniques:

Technique	Description
Stakeholder interviews	These interviews give stakeholders the opportunity to comment on the existing website. These comments should be collated for later analysis.
Feedback mechanisms	Allow visitors the opportunity to comment on your site using contact-us forms, polls, and surveys.
User testing	Watching visitors use your existing site can be enlightening. It's a powerful way to identify problems in the usability of your site.

Quantitative analysis, on the other hand, draws on various automated analytical tools that provide information about different aspects of your site's performance. These include the following:

Tool	Description
Web log analyzer	Every time a user interacts with your website, information about that interaction is stored. Analysis of these logs can help identify areas of improvement.
Automated performance checker	Automated checkers assess things like accessibility, download times, and browser support. They help maximize your audience.

Tool	Description
Q Online visibility tracker	Having a great site is important—but if nobody knows it exists, then it has failed. There are a number of ways to gain an understanding of how visible your site is online.

Let's look in more detail at these two approaches and better understand the role of each.

Qualitative feedback

I've already discussed stakeholder interviews and will cover user testing in chapter 6, "User-centric design." This section will focus on other feedback mechanisms.

Most websites provide some method by which users can submit feedback. This is normally a contact page, but something more proactive is needed if you want consistent user feedback. Most users won't think to send in comments unless they're frustrated with your site. The problem is that in such situations, users tend to leave rather than complain.

> For advice on running online surveys, read Jakob Nielsen's article "Keep Online Surveys Short" at http://www.useit.com/alertbox/20040202.html.

If you want feedback about your site, then specifically ask for it. You can do so with a simple feedback form or a more comprehensive survey. But here's a word of warning if you're considering a full-blown survey: few users take the time to complete a long questionnaire, so keep your questions to a minimum. Also avoid making your requests for feedback too intrusive—they shouldn't hinder users from completing their goals.

If you're considering making changes to an existing site, it's well worth implementing a basic feedback mechanism to canvas opinion before you begin. Whether you're getting feedback from your site through user testing or via stakeholder interviews, you need to assess the value of the comments made. When analyzing negative comments about your site use these four criteria to judge how seriously those comments need to be taken:

> How often the comment is being made

> Who makes the comment

> What affect the problem has on the user and your objectives for the site

> How easy the problem is to fix

The more often you're hearing the same negative comment, the more likely it is that the comment is justified and needs addressing. But you can't rely on numbers alone. If your biggest customer has a problem, then you had better address that concern fast!

You also need to ascertain the seriousness of each problem. Does it stop the user from completing a task, or is it simply a mild inconvenience? Does it in some way hamper a business objective? If it does, then it needs to be dealt with.

Finally, establish how difficult the problem is to fix. Even a minor problem is worth fixing if it's easy to do. Conversely, fixing a major problem may be unjustifiable if the expense is prohibitive. In such situations, look for a work-around that lessens the seriousness of the issue. Ultimately, these decisions are about return on investment. Does the seriousness of the problem justify the cost of fixing it?

Although nothing is better than feedback from your users, obtaining it can be a battle. Stakeholder interviews and user testing are time consuming, and site feedback mechanisms are often ignored. Quantitative analysis is much less work, but you should use it to support, not replace, qualitative feedback.

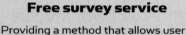

Adobe support provides a simple but unobtrusive feedback mechanism. The side column asks users if they found the support document useful..

Free survey service

Providing a method that allows user feedback doesn't have to be expensive or complicated. A number of services such as questionform.com let you create free surveys in minutes.

Quantitative analysis

At the beginning of the chapter, I talked about how bad I am at assembling flat-pack furniture. Part of my problem is that I never have the right tools. Fortunately, when it comes to analyzing the strengths and weaknesses of your site, there is no shortage of tools. Let's look at the three types of analytical tools I mentioned earlier, starting with web stats.

Traffic analysis

The best-known form of analysis is carried out on a site's log files. Log files track where a user came from, what pages they have visited, how long they spent on each page, and other data about users' interaction with your site. The problem is that log files are hard to understand. Many tools are available to help with this, from free open source software to expensive enterprise-level products.

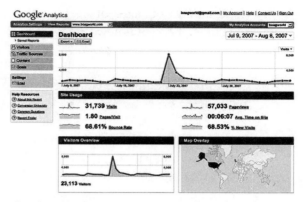

Google Analytics gathers a wealth of information about your users and how they navigate your site.

It's probably best to start with something cheap. In my experience, the majority of website owners don't use the advanced features offered by high-end tools. You can always upgrade later.

Another option is to use a statistics collector that doesn't rely on log files. One such tool is Google Analytics. It collects considerably more data than web logs and has an easy-to-use interface for analyzing the results. It's free of charge and only requires a small piece of code on each page to work.

How do you judge if an existing site is performing? You can look at three basic things:

> *The number of unique users and where they're coming from*—If many sites are linking to you, it's a good sign that you're doing something right. Traffic levels also indicate the performance of existing marketing campaigns. But here's a word of warning: large numbers of unique users don't necessarily indicate a successful site. Quality is more important than quantity.

> *The percentage of repeat visitors compared to first-time users*—If users are returning to your site regularly, it's normally a sign of satisfaction.

> *How users are moving around your site*—How long are they spending on individual pages? How many pages are they viewing? From which page are they leaving the site?

The final test is trickier to interpret. A user may visit many pages, which can appear to be a sign of interest in the site. It may also mean they can't find the information they require. Compare the time on site to the number of pages viewed. If the user looks at a good number of pages for a reasonable time, then you know things are going well.

By looking at where a user leaves, you can get an indication of potential problems. Are users only looking at your home page? If they're leaving without viewing other pages, then you have a problem with your home page. Are users getting to checkout on your e-commerce website and then giving up? Perhaps it's time to user test your checkout process.

It's easy to misinterpret website statistics. For example, a large number of page views may mean people can't find the information they're looking for.

You can do a lot more with web stats, but this should be enough for you to analyze your existing site. Let's now turn our attention to automated checkers.

Automated performance checkers

When analyzing your web stats, you may notice a significant number of users who leave your site without viewing a single page. This can be happen for a variety of reasons. They may have come to the wrong site or been confused by the user interface. But it may also mean they have met technical difficulties accessing your site.

You can easily perform three tests to identify potential problems:

> ### Automated performance tools
>
> To see what your site looks like in different browsers, try http://www.browsershots.org. To check accessibility, go to http://www.contentquality.com/. For monitoring download times. I recommend http://www.website optimization.com/services/analyze/.

> *Check your site on as many different browsers as possible.* I recommend that you look at your site in at least the last two versions of Internet Explorer, Firefox, Opera, and Safari. If you don't have access to all of these browsers, then try an online service such as BrowserShots (http://www.browsershots.org).

> *Check your site's accessibility using an online accessibility checker.* These tools provide a report outlining the various accessibility problems with your site. A word of warning: automated accessibility reports can be both misleading and confusing, as you'll discover in chapter 7, "Ensuring access for all." Nevertheless, they can help you identify possible accessibility problem with your site.

> *Carry out a speed test on your site.* Users will often abandon a site they perceive as taking too long to download. How quickly a page should load depends on the type of content and the connection speed of most users.

Automated checkers have a broader role than monitoring site performance. They can also be used to track your site's online visibility.

Online visibility trackers

Web stats and performance checkers provide information about site usability and accessibility, but they don't tell you how easy your site is to find. Fortunately, tools are available that do exactly that.

Start with a site like http://www.popuri.us. This site checks various sources to ascertain your online visibility.

If you want information about your site's ranking for specific search terms, then a tool like http://www.googlerankings.com will help. Despite the name, this free application checks all major search engines and reports your rankings for whatever terms you specify.

In addition, a number of desktop tools bring all this functionality (and more) together. For the purposes of assessing an existing site, the free online tools are adequate. Chapter 10, "Driving traffic," will discuss the need to monitor your site's visibility on an ongoing basis, especially when you're tracking marketing campaigns. In this situation, a desktop application may be more convenient.

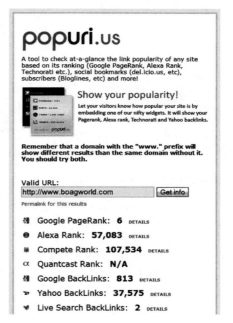

Popuri.us is a free web application that checks your site's ranking on search engines, blog listings, and social networking applications.

Of course, knowing that your site ranks 4,653 on Alexa or that 364 people link to it from del.icio.us isn't in itself that useful. The real power of online visibility trackers is that you can check on your competition as well.

CHECK OUT THE COMPETITION

Take the time to look at your competition's websites
and identify what works and what doesn't.

To assess the strengths and weaknesses of your existing site, you need to judge it in context. The best way to achieve this is to compare it with your competition.

Most organizations have a clear picture of who their competition is. Depending on your sector, this list can be long. Doing a detailed competitive analysis of everyone isn't cost efficient. I recommend keeping the analysis lightweight and selecting a small number of sites to look at (between four and six). Be careful: the tendency when narrowing the field is to focus on the largest competitors, which can be a mistake. The smaller competitors, or those new to the marketplace, are more likely to be doing something innovative, which you may be able to learn from. Try to ensure a mix of both larger and smaller sites.

Reviewing your competition

Try to review your competitor's website in a similar way to your own. Some adaptation will be required when you don't have access to information.

For example, it won't be possible to interview their internal stakeholders. You also won't be able to survey existing visitors through contact forms or online polls. Instead, you need to deploy alternative methods like user testing. Testing the competition gives you an opportunity to try responses to design, content, site structure, and functionality. You can learn from what they have done right and improve on what they have done badly. It's the perfect training ground.

Although user testing is useful, it shouldn't replace basic analysis on your part. Take time to look at your competition and ask yourself these questions:

> What message and tone of voice are used on this site?

> What content and functionality are highlighted on the home page and in the navigation?

> What image are they trying to project through the design?

> What functionality and content do they have compared to your website?

> What labeling are they applying to the content areas and site sections?

The aim is to better understand your competition's online strategy. Why have they chosen to approach a problem in a different way than you? Does that alternative approach give them an advantage? But always remember, just because a competitor's website is successful for them doesn't mean the same approach will work for you. You should learn from your competitors, not copy them blindly.

It isn't necessary to limit your analysis of the competition to qualitative methods (such as user testing). You can do quantitative analysis too.

Testing your competition

As with reviewing the competition, some adaptation is required when doing quantitative analysis. This is because you don't have access to their log files. But you can learn a lot from checking the competition's online visibility.

Do your competitors' websites rank higher than your own? Do more people link to them? Is there more talk about your competitors' brands? Who links to your competition, and can you persuade them to link to you?

To quickly find out who is linking to your competition, you can type the following into Google link:
http://www.yourCompetition.com.

Finding the answers to all these questions is simple. Use the same popuri.us service I mentioned earlier, and enter your competition's web addresses. You can also use other tools to test your competition, such as using the automated checkers to see how well built their websites are.

All these techniques should give you a clear understanding of your competition. But more important is the need to understand your users.

PICTURE YOUR USERS

Many website owners feel they have a clear picture of their users, but often they don't. When asked, their answers are vague and ill defined. "The general public" or even "women over 50" isn't well enough defined to be useful.

It's important that everybody on the web team has a clear understanding of the target audience. It has to be more than a vague idea in your head. The designer needs to understand the audience in order to create a look and feel that resonates with those users.

All members of the web team need to clearly understand the target audience.

The content providers have to know, so they can write at an appropriate reading level and use terminology the reader is familiar with. The list goes on.

Fortunately, the process of refining and communicating your target audience consists of only two painless steps. First, list and prioritize your audience. Second, create personas for each of the target groups. Let's begin by prioritizing your users.

Prioritizing your users

Make a list of users who might be interested in your site. Be specific, and include as many types as you can. You'll probably end up with a long list. It's the length of this list that spells disaster for many web projects. By targeting such a large number of diverse audiences, they inevitably end up appealing to nobody. Where they could have had a focused, engaging website, they end up with a bland solution.

It isn't wrong to have a broad audience, but the list of target users needs additional work in order to aid, rather than harm, the development process. I recommend prioritizing your audience into three groups:

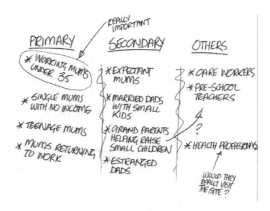

This is an initial draft of a target audience list I wrote for a health care site. The site provided advice about health issues of preschool children. The list was further refined before being given to the entire project team.

Description	
Primary	The primary audience is the group around which you focus design, content, and functionality. The aim is to maximize their user experience.
Secondary	Although the site isn't specifically tailored to the secondary audience, it still has sections designed for their needs. These appear as micro sites, landing pages, or subsections.
Others	Although the site's content caters to other audiences, the design and usability aren't focused specifically on them. That said, nothing in the site should create unnecessary difficulties.

Whether you're redesigning a whole website or producing a new piece of functionality for an existing site, list and prioritize your audience. The audience for a specific piece of functionality may be different from that of the website as a whole. For example, the primary audience for an application may be only a secondary audience for the site itself. Make sure everybody involved in the project gets a copy of the final prioritized list. Designers and copywriters in particular will find it invaluable.

But defining your users doesn't need to stop there. You can also look at creating personas.

Creating personas

A *persona* is a description of a fictional individual. You can use personas to bring more life to the audiences on your list and help you better engage with them as real individuals. A persona helps those involved in a web project to really understand the needs and motivation of your target audience. As with the audience list, personas should be distributed to all members of your team and will be key in design, copywriting, and user testing.

But probably the most valuable role that personas fulfill is to act as a reference point. After you have personified the target audience and given the persona a name, you can use it as a sanity check for development decisions.

Personas help you to focus on the needs of your users.

For example, you can ask yourself, "What would Ben think of this piece of functionality? Would he find it useful?" This helps the team to always remain focused on user needs.

How do you create a persona, and what information should it include? Let's explore an example.

A persona is a mini biography, normally confined to a single sheet of paper. Each persona relates to a user group from your target audience list. You can create as many personas as you wish. I recommend creating at least one for each of your primary audiences. For this example, we'll create a single persona based on a fictional primary audience for a health spa website.

Sample persona: "mum with young kids"

Basic information	Persona explained
Name: Jane Smith Marital status: married Age: 27  Occupation: Midwife	"Mum with young kids" doesn't help you connect with the persona. The first step in creating this connection is to give your fictional person a name: Jane Smith. Giving her a name also provides a handy way to refer to that persona.
	Next, you need to establish some basic information about Jane. She is female, age 20 to 35. Let's say 27. You also need to decide if she is in a relationship. This probably isn't vital to the persona, but it helps flesh out the character. Let's say she's married.
	Now, let's add a picture. Again, this isn't entirely necessary, but it helps bring the persona to life.
	Occupation may range hugely across your audience, but you need to pick something. Let's say Jane works part time as a midwife. This job fits nicely around her childcare requirements. It also supplements her husband's income and gives them more disposable cash.
Children: 2 (ages 18 months and 6 years)	Let's say she has two children, ages 18 months and 6 years. You don't always need to specify this information; but because children are a defining characteristic for this persona, it's worth mentioning.

Even with just this basic demographic information, you're starting to build a picture of Jane's life. You know she's busy, rushing from school to her job and back again. She has little free time and probably craves peace and quiet. Being a midwife, she is intelligent and well educated. She also has adequate disposable income to afford the health spa.

In short, she is considered an ideal candidate for the health spa. It would provide a welcome break from the kids and her hectic lifestyle. You know she has the income to afford a "treat" like this occasionally. The next step is to understand how Jane interacts with the web.

Web usage	Persona explained
Jane has little time to surf the web. Because she always has children underfoot, the internet rarely receives her full attention.	How much does this persona use the web, and what does she use it for? In the case of Jane, she probably doesn't us the web much. She isn't required to use it as part of her job, and she hardly has time at home to surf!
	Unless she is gives up her precious quiet time after the kids have gone to bed, she'll probably look at the web with children running around. Chances are, she won't be able to give the site her full attention.
Jane uses the web occasionally to find childcare information, buy clothing, and order food. She isn't uncomfortable using computers when required.	Jane is well educated, so she uses the computer occasionally to look at childcare information or as a research tool for work. She may also make purchases of clothing and groceries online, because she doesn't have time to go shopping. Beyond that, her usage is limited.

The final step is to determine what Jane will look for at the health spa website.

User requirements	Persona explained
If Jane visits the spa site, she'll probably already have decided in principle to go. She won't require much persuasion.	You know that Jane doesn't surf the web. When she does go online, she doesn't hang around. As a result, she is unlikely to stumble across the site. More likely, she came to the site via something like a brochure. She probably already knows that she wants to go to a spa by this stage. It's just a matter of which spa is right for her.
The first information Jane requires when arriving on the site is price and availability. Only then will she look at what exactly is offered.	What will make Jane choose this spa? Her primary motivations are most likely price and availability: price because with two kids, she'll feel that the trip is an extravagance; and availability because she'll have to arrange childcare. Only when these needs are shown to have been met will she allow herself to explore the site and find out how she can be pampered.
Jane needs the website to be easy to use and provide quick access to the key information she requires.	Jane is busy and can't give any website her full attention. It's therefore important that the site is easy to use and quickly tells her what she needs to know. If it doesn't, she's likely to go to a competitor's site.

Even a basic persona can provide an in-depth understanding of your audience. Personas are a great tool whose power extends well beyond the website and can even affect overall business strategy. For example, wouldn't it be helpful if the spa provided childcare, so that Jane didn't need to arrange a babysitter?

Next actions

This chapter has brought together the background information required to run a stress-free web project. But this information must be refined into something tangible. Only then can you turn it into a brief that the web developers can work from. Before moving on to the next chapter, take a moment to complete the following actions.

ACTION 1: *Collate your research.* In this chapter, you've researched organizational and site objectives, developed success criteria, and come to better understand your target audience. You've also analyzed your website and that of the competition. Take some time to condense this information into a short, digestible form. Take the ideas that have come out of stakeholder interviews, competitive analysis, and site review, and record them as a list that you can refine.

ACTION 2: *Refine by objectives.* Start refining your wish list based on your site objectives and success criteria. Does that great idea suggested in the stakeholder interviews line up with your site objectives? Will that functionality on your competition's website help you meet your success criteria? If not, remove it to a "maybe later" list.

ACTION 3: *Refine by persona needs.* After creating your persona, take your newly trimmed list and look at it from your persona's point of view. Would Jane (the fictional persona) find the idea useful? Would it help her within her day-to-day constraints? If the answer is yes, keep the item on the list. If not, remove it, but keep it safe for the future.

You should now have a definitive list that can be implemented as a web project. Combined with your personas, list of target groups, success criteria, and website objectives, you have everything you need to write a brief and assemble your team.

3

The perfect team

In this chapter

> **Choose when to outsource**

> **Clearly define your project**

> **Write an effective brief**

    Providing context

    Clearly stating your requirements

    Defining your deliverables

    Learning about the supplier

> **Avoid disasters**

    Never request speculative design

    Avoid writing a wish list

> **Select the perfect team**

    Narrowing the field

    Reading between the lines

    Making the final selection

       ■ *Assessing the proposals*

       ■ *Interviewing the short list*

       ■ *Talking to references*

I'm a huge fan of the *Mission Impossible* TV show. I loved it that each week, Ethan Hunt assembled the perfect team to complete his mission. People were carefully selected based on their skills, and each person got their moment of glory when their specialty saved the team. From the prosthetics artist to the explosives expert, every person played their part.

Of course, the heroes in these stories were only trying to complete an impossible mission. They certainly weren't doing anything as challenging as building a website! They instinctively knew the plan for success and who could help them complete it. Unfortunately, in the real world, things are much tougher.

In chapter 2, "Stress-free planning," you established an outline of what needed to be done to complete your project. Now that outline must be turned into an actionable plan. You need to assemble your team and brief them properly. How do you find the right people? How do you ensure that your team knows exactly what is expected of them?

In this chapter, we'll look at how to write a *brief* (also known as a *scope of work*) and select your team. But first, you need to make one vital decision: are you going to develop your web project in-house or outsource it to an external web agency?

CHOOSE WHEN TO OUTSOURCE

In many situations, the decision to develop in-house or outsource isn't up to you. Either an internal team already exists, or you're forced to outsource because you can't fund in-house staff. What if you have that choice? How do you decide between developing your website in-house or outsourcing to an external agency? Let's compare the choices:

Using an internal web team	Outsourcing to a web-design agency
Internal teams are more cost effective for *long-term projects* and ongoing maintenance.	Outsourcing is more cost effective for *short projects* where the expenses of hiring, salary, training, and equipment would be prohibitive for an in-house team.
In-house teams work within the business, so they can *understand organizational objectives* and the target audience better than an external agency.	An external agency brings a *fresh perspective* that an institutionalized in-house team can't offer.
An internal team is *committed to evolving the website* over time. They're constantly looking for ways to improve the site.	External agencies have a *broader perspective* of the whole industry, rather than only what is happening within a single company.
An in-house team is able to *promote the website internally* and ensure that it doesn't become neglected.	An external agency needs to constantly ensure that it's *cutting edge* to stay competitive. This guarantees that the quality of work is consistently high.
Because an internal team isn't juggling multiple clients, they can (if well managed) be *more responsive* than an external agency.	Because external agencies tend to be larger than in-house teams, they have *more specialized and highly skilled staff.*

Your choice comes down to the length of the project and the funding available. If your website needs constant development and will evolve on an ongoing basis, then an in-house team may be more appropriate. Of course, supporting an in-house team can be expensive.

You must consider the initial costs of recruitment and equipment, and the ongoing expenses of salary and training. For shorter development projects, the benefits and cost savings of outsourcing may outweigh the convenience of an in-house team.

In reality, there is no reason why you can't combine both approaches. You could use an external agency for development work while ongoing maintenance was handled by an internal web editor. Equally, you could do the bulk of development internally but bring in external agencies for specialist work such as search-engine optimization. This hybrid approach combines the strengths of both in-house and external.

Whatever your approach, you'll need to provide a brief from which people can work.

CLEARLY DEFINE YOUR PROJECT

Having a clearly written, well-defined *scope of work* (or *brief*) is central to a successful web project, especially when you engage an external agency. The length of your brief should reflect the size and complexity of the project. It should also reflect the audience toward whom it's aimed. For example, a brief that is distributed to external agencies needs more background information than one aimed at in-house developers.

Although it's tempting not to write a brief for smaller projects, skipping this step will cause problems further down the line. All projects should have some kind of brief.

The desire to avoid writing a brief can be strong, especially for a smaller project that's being developed internally. I encourage you to always write a brief, no matter what the circumstances, because a brief provides many benefits:

> *Limits scope creep*—Projects without a brief lack definition and allow new functionality to be added on the fly. This results in slippages and loss of direction.

> *Improves costing accuracy*— Whether you're developing in-house or outsourcing, a project needs to be costed. Costs include expenditures on external agencies, or time and salary for in-house staff.

If you choose to ask external agencies to respond to your brief, allow time for them to ask questions. Don't send out your brief and then go on vacation until after the deadline for responses!

> *Clearly defines tasks*—A well-written brief enables your development team to identify specifically what tasks need to be completed and by whom.

> *Specifies delivery dates*—When tasks are established, it becomes easier to estimate how long the project will take. If this exceeds the specified deadline, then additional resources are required.

> *Provides context for the developers*—A good brief includes background research (see chapter 1, "The secret to a successful website"), which encourages intelligent suggestions.

> *Sets expectations*—A brief explains to the developers exactly what is expected and ensures that internal stakeholders understand the scope of the project. This avoids disappointment and disputes further down the line.

> *Improves communication*—A good brief should stimulate discussion between yourself and the developers. When you distribute it, expect questions and encourage feedback.

We have established that a scope of work is important. But what goes into it?

WRITE AN EFFECTIVE BRIEF

There is no single way to write a web-design brief. It depends on who will be reading the brief and on the size of the project. A short email may suffice for a internal developer adding a contact form to a site. For a website redesign or new sub-site, a larger document is required. Although the complexity of a brief varies, four broad categories of elements should appear:

> Context

> Requirements

> Deliverables

> Information about the developer

Let's begin with context.

Providing context

An effective brief should provide background information about the project, drawn from the research you gathered in chapter 2. The amount of context required depends on the reader's knowledge. If the document is being sent to external agencies, then more context is required. Less is needed for an internal audience that is aware of this background information.

Consider the needs of your reader. Information should be distributed on a "need to know" basis. No matter the size of the project, always include the following:

> *Target audience*—For smaller projects, list the target audience and what they want to achieve. For larger projects, include the personas you developed in chapter 2.

> *About your organization*—When you're using an external agency for the first time, provide background information about who you are and what you do. Don't give them the company history. Instead, focus on

On smaller projects, cover the key areas of context but in less detail.

your mission statement, your organizational objectives, and how you use the web to achieve your goals.

> *Aims and objectives*—The emphasis of any brief should be on the project objectives. State what the project should achieve and how that goal will be measured. These are the success criteria you created in chapter 2.

> *Competition*—Provide information about your competitors, especially when they have functionality that's similar to what you're developing. On large projects, also include the competitive reviews you completed in chapter 2.

Clearly stating your requirements

The majority of your brief should outline project requirements. This includes any limitations such as budget or time scales.

Let's look at an example that demonstrates these requirements: a fictional e-commerce site called The Joke Factory. This site sells practical-joke merchandise but now also wishes to offer electronic gift certificates. Here's a sample requirements section for this project:

Content of the brief	Explanation of the approach
The Joke Factory wants to enable its e-commerce site to support electronic gift certificates. Certificates appear as products and come in three values ($10, $25, $50). Users can add these certificates to their basket. After the order has been confirmed, the user enters a personal message and email address for the recipient. The message is sent to the email address along with a unique code that can be entered at checkout. This code applies the discount. A confirmation of the email's delivery is also sent to the purchaser. This functionality is similar to that provided by amazon.com. Any suggestions about the specifics of how the functionality should work are welcome.	*Outline the functionality required.* Explain how it works by outlining the user experience. What will the user see? What can they do? How will the site respond? Use examples if possible. Note the reference to amazon.com. This helps the developers visualize what is required. Encourage suggestions from the developers. It's good practice to allow developers to suggest alternative approaches. A web project should be a collaborative process between website owner and developers.
The new gift-certificate system should integrate with our existing website. This site is built using Classic ASP with a SQL Server 2007 database. The front end is built using the latest standards-based techniques.	*Communicate any technical constraints.* This prevents the developers from suggesting inappropriate solutions. Don't worry if the wording here sounds like gibberish. Many of the terms will be explained later in the book. If in doubt, ask your existing developers to outline any technical considerations that should be included.
The selection of gift certificates should closely reflect the process of choosing other products. The form field that lets users redeem their vouchers should be clearly explained and consistent with the rest of the checkout process. Finally, the certificate emails should be visually attractive and conform to corporate guidelines (see attached).	*Describe any design specifications.* If you have a style guide, refer to that. Also mention other sites that convey the look you want. But be specific about which elements you like and why.

Content of the brief	Explanation of the approach
After this new service is launched, we wish to promote it with our existing customers. We require the creation of a promotional email and distribution of that email to our mailing list. The list of email addresses can be provided in an Excel document and consists of just under 10,000 addresses.	*List requirements beyond design and build.* These can include things like email marketing, search-engine optimization, and hosting. The requirements segment should outline these items to avoid unforeseen costs further down the line.
The Joke Factory's sales are seasonable with the peak at Christmas. We therefore want the new gift-certificate functionality available by late October.	*Discuss deadlines.* Don't create artificial deadlines. Doing so will limit the number of agencies tendering. Include legitimate deadlines, and explain why they exist.
We have allocated $5,000 for this project. But we'll accept higher bids if they can be justified. Although cost is an important factor in our decision, it isn't the only consideration. The ability to meet deadlines and integrate into our existing site is also very important.	*Include an indication of budget.* Any web project can be approached in different ways, and without an indication of budget, the web developer won't know the most suitable. Also indicate how important the budget is in your decision. Will you consider responses to your brief that exceed your budget, or will you accept the cheapest quote?

Many website owners are suspicious about revealing their budget, but talking about budget is an important part of the tendering process.

Did the last section of the table make you uncomfortable? Many website owners feel that disclosing their budget encourages agencies to mark up the value of the project.

If you disclose your budget, you'll see many responses come in just under, but this isn't because of overcharging. There are many ways to fulfill a brief, and budget dictates the quality of the approach taken. The more funds available, the better the solution that can be provided.

It's similar to buying a car. Both a Yugo and a Ferrari get you from A to B, but one is better quality than the other. Also, when buying a car, you choose extras like air conditioning and GPS. Your budget constrains what you select. In the same way, if the web-design agency knows your budget, this informs what extras they propose for your site and the quality of the build. A higher budget lets developers spend more time on user testing and accessibility requirements.

As with cars, the quality of solution is dictated by the budget available.

Most website owners don't have the experience to know what a reasonable budget is, but they *do* know a project's worth to their business. The Joke Factory should know how many gift certificates they anticipate selling. They know their profit on each sale and so can estimate the revenue they expect to generate. This should help them develop a budget for the project. If the quotes that come back vastly exceed the budget, then the project can't be justified. Not all projects are so easy to price, but the budget can't be ignored. Set an approximate figure based on funds available, but encourage agencies not to be too constrained by this figure.

Requirements focus on functionality and design, but we also need to cover issues of quality and ownership by defining deliverables.

Defining your deliverables

The quality of what is delivered can vary hugely depending on the available time and budget. Problems arise when the various parties have different perceptions of what the deliverables should be. The following three areas can cause particular conflict:

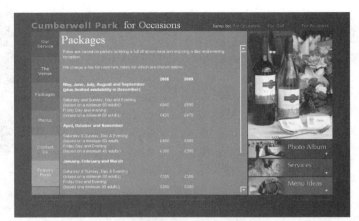

A badly built website can look fine on one browser and be unusable in another.

Internet Explorer

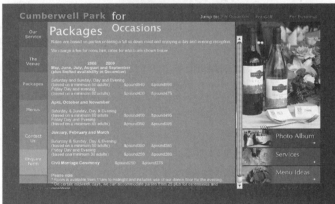

Safari

> *Standard of code*—Not all website code is created equal. To keep costs low, some web-design agencies take shortcuts. Others are unaware of web design best practice. Make sure you specify your requirements when writing the brief. In chapter 7, "Ensuring access for all," we'll explore what those requirements should be. But not all projects need to conform to the latest standards; in some situations, a quick and dirty approach is a necessary evil. The important thing is that everybody has the same expectations.

> *Accessibility of the deliverable*—Although browser support isn't strictly to do with accessibility, it's a related subject and one that is extremely contentious. State up front which browsers you want your site tested on. As a minimum, specify the last two versions of Internet Explorer and the latest versions of Safari, Firefox,

and Opera. Consider support for alternatives devices such as screen readers and cell phones. Remember, extensive browser testing will affect budget. It's therefore important to balance accessibility with return on investment. Accessibility also extends beyond browser issues, as we'll explore in chapter 7.

> *Ownership of assets*—You must specify two types of ownership. First are assets created as part of the development process. Who owns the Photoshop files used to create the look and feel? What about the source files for any Flash applications created? Although it isn't necessary to own these files, not owning them can cause problems if you wish to use a different agency in the future. The second type of ownership involve intellectual property. If the agency develops an animated character for use on your website, do you have the rights to use it in TV commercials or print work? Lay out your requirements in the brief. Many agencies charge more for ownership, and you need to know these costs ahead of time.

After you've set the deliverables, requirements, and context for your brief, the developers have all they need to provide a quote. If you're using an external agency, you should request background information about the agency itself.

Learning about the supplier

One advantage of an in-house team is that you know them. Even if you haven't worked with the individuals before, you know about the organization they work for and can easily canvas opinion about their competence. But with external agencies, that kind of information is harder to acquire.

It's often hard to tell how trustworthy an external agency is.

If you choose to use an external agency, every proposal you receive will include information about the agency. Although this sales copy does have value, you can't rely on it. You must dig deeper by asking for specific information in your brief. Here are a few questions that will prove enlightening:

If you're seeking a long-term partnership with an
external agency, be sure of their financial security.

Question to ask	What the question reveals
How many years has your agency been in business?	Younger companies can suffer from problems in their workflow and delivery.
Can you provide accounts for the last three years?	Viewing the financial accounts of an agency indicates how likely the company is to be around for ongoing support.
How many staff members do you employ, and what is the approximate makeup of responsibilities?	The size and makeup of an organization helps determine if they can successfully deliver your project. Even a large agency will struggle to deliver a technical project if the majority of their staff are designers.
Can you provide resumes for key staff who may potentially be involved on our project?	Don't expect an agency to be able to tell you the final project team, but ask for resumes anyway.
What liability insurance does your company hold that may be relevant to this project?	An agency may fail to deliver, or work can be lost for some reason. Having financial recompense available is a reassuring safety net.

Along with these questions, always ask for references. References are an invaluable way of learning more about the agency, as you'll discover later in this chapter.

Finally, ask for examples of relevant work. This shows the quality of the developers' work and their experience on similar projects. Website owners often fail to do this when engaging an agency to do design work. Instead, they ask the agency to produce a number of design mockups, which is a flawed approach.

AVOID DISASTERS

What should you avoid doing when writing a brief? I could mention many mistakes, but I want to focus on two: requesting speculative designs and writing a wish list rather than a brief.

Never request speculative design

Speculative design means a client asks an agency to provide initial design mockups to support their tender. Requesting design work up front seems like a good idea; it provides an opportunity to assess an external agency's design skills and has become common practice. By association, many companies think it must be best practice.

Unfortunately, the supposed benefits are misleading, and there are good reasons for avoiding speculative design:

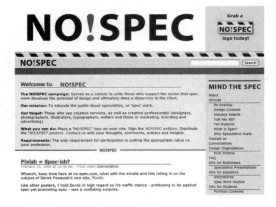

NO!SPEC (http://www.no-spec.com/) campaigns against speculative design, claiming that it "ultimately does a disservice to the client."

> *Speculative design favors superficiality.* Good design is a collaborative process between agency and client. The agency needs to have a full grasp of brand, business drivers, and user requirements. The design emerges after numerous iterations and multiple rounds of user testing. Speculative design doesn't allow for this, instead relying solely on which agency can draw the prettiest picture.

Would you have hired the designer who created this web page? Probably not, because although it's usable, it lacks the "wow" factor.

> *Speculative design focuses on the client, not the user.* Good design is about facilitating the user and enabling them to complete tasks easily. A good agency challenges a client's perception of design, focusing them on user needs. Speculative design exists only to impress the client. It encourages agencies to focus on winning your work, not on making tough design decisions.

> *Successful agencies won't do speculative design.* Speculative design is expensive for agencies. It's perceived as a sign that the client wants something for nothing. If an agency is successful and has no trouble generating work, they tend not to respond to briefs that include speculative design. A willingness to produce speculative design can be a sign of a new or struggling agency.

> *You pay for speculative design.* The perception that no cost is associated with requesting speculative design is false. The agency has to cover its cost of sale by adding it onto the projects it wins. In the end, clients pay not only for the speculative designs produced for their project, but also for other projects the agency failed to win.

Later in this chapter, we'll cover alternative ways of assessing an agency's design skills. For now, it's enough to put a requirement in your brief to see examples of related work.

Speculative design isn't the only mistake you can make when writing a brief.

Avoid writing a wish list

A brief can turn into a wish list of functionality rather than immediate requirements. Even after refining your ideas according to users' needs and business requirements, you may still have an extensive list of work that needs to be done.

The best approach is to break requirements into mini-projects (or *modules*) that can be rolled out over time. This *phased development* provides a number of benefits:

It is hard to provide accurate quotes
for price and timescales on large projects.

> *Increases speed of delivery*—Some modules can be launched while others are in development. This prevents a single module from stalling the entire rollout.

> *Leads to more accurate estimates*—Bigger project are harder to estimate. Breaking them down makes it easier for suppliers to quote accurately.

> *Improves cash flow*—Phased development spreads the cost of a project. Instead of having two or three large payments, you have a number of smaller payments associated with the delivery of each micro-project.

> *Provides PR opportunities*—Whenever a new feature is launched, you have an opportunity to publicize your site. New features can motivate users into taking another look. A single large project provides only a single opportunity to grab people's attention.

> *Limits the risks of working with a new supplier*—Choosing an agency is always a risk. Until you work with somebody, it's hard to gauge how good they are. Reduce this risk by limiting the size of project they're commissioned to build. If the agency fails to perform, you can look elsewhere when commissioning subsequent work.

Unfortunately, it isn't always possible to break projects into modules. Sometimes you have to commission an agency for an entire project. In such situations, it's important that you select the right team.

SELECT THE PERFECT TEAM

If you choose to outsource, selecting a web-design agency is a crucial step in the web-development process. The wrong decision can have devastating consequences on your project, leading to considerable stress and delays.

Not every website owner faces this challenge. Many work with existing in-house teams. But there are number of reasons why a website owner with an in-house team may still choose to outsource.

Who, then, do you invite to tender? How do you evaluate their proposals and presentations?

Narrowing the field

After days of research, refinement, and crafting, you finally have the perfect web-design brief. With millions of web-design companies worldwide, who do you send it to?

One option is to filter by geography. There are valid reasons for selecting a web-design agency in your country. Issues such as currency, time zones, and corporate law can make working with international agencies challenging. But beyond that, geography has little effect. An agency is just as capable of developing your project whether it's next door or a thousand miles away.

If a website doesn't provide the information you require, phone the agency directly. A five-minute phone call can be more enlightening than poring over a site for hours.

Methods for finding web design agencies

Worst selection method
Random Google search
Selected based on geography
Selected based on work in similar sector
Selected because they designed a site you like
Recommended in a form or mailing list
Recommended by a trade association
Recommenede by a trusted contact

Best selection method

Some methods for finding web-design agencies are more successful than others.

The best approach is word-of-mouth recommendations, especially from somebody you know and respect. Start by talking to your suppliers or other business partners. Who did they use to build their site? What was their experience like? If you're part of a trade association, see if they have any recommendations. Also, ask for recommendations in any forums or mailing lists related to your sector.

Finally, look at websites that you like or consider successful. Most sites have a link to the agency that developed them. If they don't, then a search on Google often reveals the agency's name. But be careful if you adopt this approach—looking at a website doesn't tell the whole story. The underlying technology may be in shambles, the management may have been appalling, and the project may have exceeded its budget and missed specified deadlines. Call the website owner first and get their opinion of the agency.

By combining these approaches, you should have a considerable list of agencies. How many you choose to send the brief to depends on the size of project and the time available. Invite too many, and you have lots of proposals to read and presentations to sit through. Invite too few, and you may not receive enough responses to do a fair comparison. For an average website redesign (if there is such a thing), anywhere from 5 to 10 is a good number. How then do you refine your list to this reasonable range?

Reading between the lines

The most effective way to refine your list of agencies is to look at their websites. An agency's website can tell you a lot about whether they're right for your project. The problem is that they're well aware of this and put considerable effort into projecting the correct image. Your challenge is to look beyond the superficial gloss. It's easy to get seduced by alluring graphics and exciting animation, but you should focus on four questions:

The size of an organization doesn't always equal adequate capacity.

1. *Do they have the capacity?* Is their team big enough, and does it have the right skill to deliver your project? To help you make that judgment, a good agency ensures that information about the size and makeup of its company is available.

2. *Do they have experience?* Agencies with experience working on similar projects or in the same sector are invaluable. This dramatically reduces the learning curve and affects costs and time scales.

3. *Can they produce the right design style?* The chosen agency must be able to design an interface that reflects your brand identity and appeals to your users. Most agencies show examples of their work on their websites. Look for examples that are aimed at a similar target audience or mirror your branding. Failing that, make sure they demonstrate a broad range of styles. If all their sites have a house style, and that isn't inline with your requirements, look elsewhere.

4. *Can they deliver your technical requirements?* Increasingly, web projects involve complex development work. An agency's site should demonstrate a capability to deliver these kinds of projects. Look for examples that are comparable to your site and use similar technologies.

This approach will allow you to create a definitive list of agencies you wish to invite to tender. After you send the brief, expect agencies to call with questions. Be sure to note the calls you receive. Who asked intelligent questions, and who hadn't read the brief thoroughly? These are all clues that help you build up a picture of the agency and aid your decision-making process.

With their questions answered, agencies should now be able to produce a detailed proposal. The next step is to choose the winning agency.

Making the final selection

Choosing an agency is an intimidating decision. But you can make the final choice using three simple steps:

1. Assess the proposals.

2. Interview the short list.

3. Talk to references.

Let's start narrowing the field by looking at the proposals you've received.

Assessing the proposals

Proposals can vary dramatically in price, approach, and technology. Without clear assessment criteria, it can seem impossible to compare the different options. Before reading the proposals, write a list of criteria by which you'll assess them. If appropriate, add weighting to important criteria. But be careful not to overweight a single category. For example, it's dangerous to put too much emphasis on price, because it can lead to a poor-quality solution.

There are no set criteria by which you should judge a proposal. The particulars of your web project dictate the criteria. But here are some you should consider:

Never dismiss a good proposal based on a single criterion. Speak to the agency and see if you can reach a compromise.

> *Understanding of the brief*—Have they understood your objectives in the solution they have proposed? Have they responded to the constraints of the brief?

> *Proven track record*—Has the agency shown examples similar to your project and using similar technologies?

> *Evidence of best practice*—Does the agency demonstrate experience in usability (see chapter 6, "User-centric design"), accessibility, and web standards (see chapter 7)?

> *Understanding of the sector*—Has the agency worked with other clients in similar sectors? Does it understand the challenges of your sector?

> *Innovation*—Has the agency challenged the brief in places and offered alternative solutions that better meet your business needs?

> *Value for the money*—Does the agency offer both value for the money and quality?

Using this approach, narrow the number of agencies to three or four. Next, arrange to meet with the remaining agencies.

Interviewing the short list

I recommend this step for all but the smallest projects. How many agencies you interview is subjective, but keep the number small. Interview too many, and they will blur together. Sitting through endless presentations is exhausting for you and unfair to the agency that gets the last slot of the day!

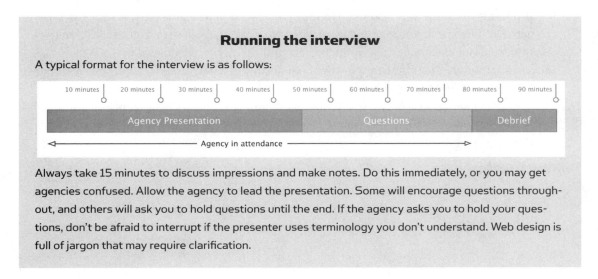

Running the interview

A typical format for the interview is as follows:

| 10 minutes | 20 minutes | 30 minutes | 40 minutes | 50 minutes | 60 minutes | 70 minutes | 80 minutes | 90 minutes |

| Agency Presentation | Questions | Debrief |

◄———————————————— Agency in attendance ————————————————►

Always take 15 minutes to discuss impressions and make notes. Do this immediately, or you may get agencies confused. Allow the agency to lead the presentation. Some will encourage questions throughout, and others will ask you to hold questions until the end. If the agency asks you to hold your questions, don't be afraid to interrupt if the presenter uses terminology you don't understand. Web design is full of jargon that may require clarification.

Inform the agencies of any requirements you have for their presentations, as well as the time available to them. One condition worth setting is who should attend. Often, an agency will only send sales staff. But it isn't the salesperson you'll be working with, so ask that at least one member of the proposed development team attend. On large projects, ask for the project manager. On smaller ones, ask for a designer or developer. This allows you to see what the working relationship might be like.

Although this is an effective approach, it can backfire. As with speculative design, some successful agencies will turn away clients who ask development staff to attend presentations. These agencies are too busy to spare staff to attend sales meetings. Use this approach only if you're concerned about the working relationship with an agency.

Remember, it isn't the sales person you'll be working with. Ask to meet the development team.

Establishing whether you can work with an agency is important. Do they approach problems the same way you do? Do they share your values and passions for the project? Do they speak your language, or does what they say go over your head? Are they honest about the challenges in the project and their own weaknesses?

Judging whether you can work with an agency is a personal decision. But meeting the agencies will help you narrow the selection to one or two agencies.

If you can't choose between two agencies, follow up on their references. This will help you make the final selection. Even if you've made a decision, still talk to references, just in case.

Talking to references

If you know what to ask, speaking to existing clients is more informative than any presentation or proposal. Take the time to call references and cover the following topics:

> *Project manager*—Ask to speak with clients who have worked with the project manager assigned to you. Discuss what the working relationship was like and how smoothly the project ran.

> *Type of work undertaken*—Agencies often exaggerate their involvement in a project to appear experienced. Clarify their role, especially when multiple suppliers were involved.

> *Approach to design*—Was the design process collaborative? Was the client's opinion valued? Were there multiple designs and iterations? Did the agency respond positively to criticisms and user feedback? Was the agency overly protective or inflexible about design?

When you talk to references, ask specifically about the project manager assigned to your project.

> *Deadlines and budget*—Being confident that an agency can deliver on its promises is the cornerstone to a successful working relationship.

> *Weaknesses*—An agency won't refer you to a disgruntled client. To avoid an entirely glowing report, ask directly about negative characteristics.

> *Approach to projects*—Was the approach flexible enough to accommodate change? Did the client speak directly to development staff, or were they confined to liaising with a project manager?

> *Ongoing support*—Did the agency respond quickly to bugs in their work? Did hidden costs emerge post-launch? Was the agency quick to respond to requests for additional functionality? Was it proactive in suggesting future developments for the site? Are the agency and the client still talking?

Covering these topics should provide the information and confidence you need to make a final selection. Now, all you need to do is finalize details and begin the project in earnest.

Next actions

In this chapter, we looked at how to engage an external web design agency. We investigated the process of writing a brief and selecting an agency. Whether you're using an internal team or an external agency, you should now be ready to start work. Before you leap into production, make sure you do the following:

ACTION 1: *Produce a statement of work.* A statement of work outlines the deliverables for your project and forms the basis of the contract. It's distinct from the briefing document, which outlines potential requirements. Instead, the statement of work describes the final product and work required to produce it. Normally, this is drawn up by the external agency; but if the work is being done in-house, then it will fall to the website owner to write it.

ACTION 2: *Have a kickoff meeting.* Meet with your team to discuss the details of the project. This meeting should include developers, designers, website owner, project manager, copywriter, and anybody else who will contribute to the final deliverables. If you've engaged an external agency, this meeting will be run by them. But if you're developing the project in-house, you'll need to call this meeting yourself. Use your brief as a rough agenda. Discuss exactly what needs to be produced, and allow those attending to ask questions. The aim is to produce a list of deliverables that everyone agrees on.

With the kickoff meeting over and statement of work produced, production can start. This book won't take you through every part of the production process, because it varies too much depending on the work being done. But in the next few chapters, I'll highlight some of the areas where you as website owner are most engaged and important information you need to know.

Let's start with the most contentious area of all: design.

4

Differences over design

In this chapter

W hy does the iPod dominate the MP3 player market? The technology is nothing special, and iPods have fewer features than many of their competitors. What makes them stand out is the user experience. The physical design of the hardware is sleek, simple, and attractive. The user interface on the device is intuitive and clean. Apple understands the power of design.

When it comes to the web, design is no less important. Nothing is more frustrating than a badly designed site.

Good design can be equally powerful. A well-designed interface guides you to the content you need, encourages a positive feeling towards a brand, and seduces you into completing calls to action.

Get the user experience wrong, and the project may fail, no matter how good the content or functionality. No wonder design is one of the most contentious and stressful parts of the development process.

TOO MANY COOKS: SUBJECTIVE DESIGN

We all have different perceptions of what makes good design. More accurately, we all have different perceptions of what makes *bad* design. Good design is to some extent invisible.

Perceptions are shaped by many factors. Personality, culture, childhood experiences, emotional state, physical surroundings, and even our own bodies dictate how you respond to design. The slightest change in a design can alter your perception of whether it's good.

Design tends to generate strong reactions, much more so than other aspects of web development. The role of design is to engage with you emotionally. The danger is that by tapping into your emotions, it may generate the wrong type of response.

Design is both subjective and divisive. This makes the job of the designer extremely challenging.

If design is both subjective and divisive, how do you successfully develop a good user experience? To a large extent, this comes down to the expertise of your designer. But producing a design is a collaborative process between designer and website owner. You're crucial in the decision-making process. These four techniques make the creation of a design less subjective and divisive:

> Focus on your target audience.

> Test designs.

> Avoid design by committee.

> Maintain a broad overview.

Let's address each in turn.

Focusing on your target audience

That crucial moment has come. The designer reveals their first design for your new web project. How will you react? Your first reaction will be personal. What do *you* think of the design? Do you like the colors, the layout, the imagery? It's impossible to react any way other than personally, but the important thing is what you do next.

One response is to start asking for changes that meet your personal aesthetic. The other reaction is to begin worrying about how others will perceive the design. For example, how will your boss react?

Both of these responses are valid. You're the person who will live and work with this design. If you aren't enthusiastic about it, then how can you expect anybody else to be? Equally, the opinions of other stakeholders are important. Getting buy-in from across the organization and making sure business objectives are reflected is a definite consideration. But neither of these responses should be the primary gauge for the success of a design.

The most important question is, what will your target audience think? The primary role of a design is to facilitate and enthuse users. It should enable them to quickly reach content while drawing them deeper into the site and engaging them with your brand. Most of all, you're endeavoring to create a positive emotional response.

One way to ascertain what your target audience thinks about a design is to refer back to the personas created in chapter 2, "Stress-free planning." How will the people in your personas react to the design? Will the design enable them to quickly find the content they need? If they're elderly, will they be able to read the text? If they're unfamiliar with computers, will they understand the interface? Try to guess how they will respond emotionally to the design. You may be able to make an educated guess based on other sites you know your target audience likes.

The ideal approach is to ask users directly about a design. But how should you do that? How can you test a design?

Assessing a design concept isn't about your personal opinion or that of your colleagues. It's about meeting the needs of your users.

Testing your design

A lot has been written about usability testing, and we'll cover that in chapter 6, "User-centric design." But little has been written about design testing. Some in the design community feel that testing undermines their role as designers. I believe that putting a design in front of real users helps to make the process less subjective and aids the sign-off process.

Cultural considerations

When you're thinking about design, don't dismiss culture just because your site has a local focus. We live in a multicultural society, and cultural considerations apply as much to your neighbors as to people around the world. Your cultural background has an affect on how you perceive a design. Color in particular can be heavily influenced by culture. For example, red is perceived as dangerous and aggressive in the West, but it's seen as a symbol of good fortune in some Eastern cultures.

Images of people need careful thought. If, for example, you wish to reach an Islamic audience, then ensure the models aren't dressed inappropriately for that culture.

What is design testing?

Design testing isn't like polling. It isn't a matter of selecting the design that scores the highest. It's an interpretative process where observation and intuition are more important than statistical results.

The most common question I use in design testing is, "Why?" By continually asking users "Why?" you dig deeper, encouraging people to express in more detail their response to a design. By talking to them face to face, you pick up their body language and emotional responses.

When working on the University of Portsmouth website, I was unsure about the design. It seemed too brash and busy. But it tested well with the 16- to 18-year-old target audience. I had to set aside my personal opinion.

Design testing also isn't like a focus group. You must engage with users on a one-to-one basis. Group discussions lead to less-confident members being influenced in their thoughts, which undermines the results. Interacting with a website is usually a solitary experience, and the design should be assessed the same way.

What happens in a design test session?

How to run design testing

Normally, users are asked to participate in two exercises:

> *Flash testing* is used to judge the hierarchy and emphasis of the design. Do users notice key content, or are they distracted by less important elements? You show users the design for a few seconds and ask them to recall as many items as they can. The tester notes both the items spotted and the order in which they're re-called. Screen elements that have the most impact are mentioned first.

> *Emotional evaluation* is an exercise where the user is asked to describe the site using non-design-related words. Phrases like "too bright" or "too busy" aren't acceptable, but "overwhelming" and "funky" are. Because personal preference varies, asking people what they think of a design is pointless. These questions trigger comments like "I don't like the green." But asking how a design makes users *feel* removes some of these distractions.

The emotional-evaluation exercise takes practice to get right. One approach is to offer users extremes to choose between. For example, is the design conservative or progressive? Is it cold or friendly? Although you're leading the user in their choice of words, the data is still useful, and the technique gets them thinking the right way. They're often able to continue unaided.

Design testing gives you concrete user opinions to feed into the decision-making process. This is important when multiple people are involved in signing off on a design and you're in danger of designing by committee.

Although users will insist on expressing their likes and dislikes, try to focus them on what impression the design leaves.

Avoiding design by committee

Design by committee is the nail in the coffin of many good design concepts. Each person has an opinion, and the design is tweaked to ensure that everyone's concerns are addressed. This creates an unobtrusive design that offends nobody but fails to excite anyone.

A mediocre design can be usable and meet the needs of your target audience. But it won't create brand loyalty, generate a feeling of satisfaction, or differentiate you from the competition.

Try to limit the number of people making design decisions. Ideally, the decision should be made by just the designer and the website owner. In the real world of internal politics, there is often a requirement to consult with others—but consultation differs from designing by committee.

The key to success is getting all parties to agree on a process before any design work begins. The following order of events works well:

Design by committee leads to uninspiring, mediocre design.

Step toward design sign-off	People involved
1. Produce initial design concepts.	Designer
2. Refine the initial concepts using business objectives and personas.	Designer and website owner
3. Present the refined design to stakeholders individually.	Designer, website owner, and stakeholders
4. Collate the responses from stakeholders, and make amendments where appropriate.	Designer and website owner
5. Present design concepts to real users.	Designer, website owner, and users
6. Collate the responses from users, and create the final iteration of the design concept.	Designer and website owner
7. Present the final design to all stakeholders together with the results of user testing and stakeholder interviews.	Designer, website owner, and stakeholders
8. Sign off on the design.	Website owner

The crucial step is the individual meetings with stakeholders. By meeting with them individually, you prevent *design on the fly*. This happens when a group of people start making changes to a design in an attempt to reach a consensus. By meeting with people one on one, you ensure that no design decisions are made in the room.

When you present a design to stakeholders, provide them with enough information to give educated feedback. Talk through the personas and objectives for the project. Ask how they believe the target audience would react to the design. Encourage them to think beyond personal preferences and focus on business and user requirements. By the time the stakeholders see the final design, they will already feel invested in it. They have

> Contributed to the process

> Been given all the background information

> Seen the design testing results

> Been educated to think from the user's perspective

You'll have done everything possible to ensure that the design isn't produced by committee. The only danger remaining is that you may personally lose objectivity.

Maintaining a broad overview

It's important to understand the difference between your role and the designer's role in the development of a site's aesthetic. It's easy for the website owner to take on the role of designer, reducing the designer to a technician who manipulates pixels.

This happens when the website owner focuses on details rather than maintaining a broad overview. The website owner should champion the needs of users and the business rather than decide how the design should work. This may appear to be a meaningless distinction—after all, the design directly affects the needs of the users and business. But there is a difference:

It's the website owner's role to focus on business and user requirements. The designer should decide how those apply to design.

Wrong type of feedback	Right type of feedback
"I hate the black and red colors. Use pink instead."	"I'm not sure our female users will like those masculine, aggressive colors."
"The layout is all wrong. Move the inquiries to the top of the page, and make it bigger."	"Our main business objective is to generate more inquiries. I think we need more emphasis on that."
"Make the logo bigger."	"We're a new company, and we need people to remember us. Can you place more emphasis on branding us strongly?"

It's the website manager's role to identify problems. The designer should propose the solution. If you solve the problem, then the designer doesn't get to understand the underlying issues and can't propose alternative solutions.

Failing to maintain this distinction undermines your relationship with the designer and wastes money. You should pay a designer for their knowledge of design principles, not just their ability to manipulate pixels. Most designers have an extensive knowledge of color theory, grid systems, visual hierarchy, and many other aspects of design. By getting heavily involved in the detail of design, you're paying them to do nothing!

The designer needs to recognize your superior understanding of the business requirements and sector. In turn, you need to recognize the designer's skills in the principles of good design. Design should be a collaborative process, and nowhere is this more important than when you're working on the design of the home page.

By explaining the underlying problem, the website owner empowers the designer to make positive suggestions that improve the design.

THE FIGHT FOR HOME-PAGE REAL ESTATE

The home page is perceived as the most important part of a website. It's common to see factions within an organization fighting to ensure that their interests are represented on the home page. In this fight for real estate, usability and design aesthetics are the first casualties. Home-page designs quickly become cluttered and unattractive as various content elements vie for attention.

Left unchecked, competition for home-page space can destroy both usability and design.

Competition for home-page space causes projects to slip and disputes to erupt. But it doesn't need to be this way. By implementing three simple techniques, you can reduce (although admittedly not eliminate) the conflict over home-page design:

> Explain the changing role of the home page.

> Avoid rushing into home-page design.

> Communicate the importance of simplicity.

Let's look in more detail at these in turn.

Understanding the changing role of the home page

Jakob Nielsen, in his book *Prioritizing Web Usability* (New Rider, 2006), writes about a change in the way users interact with the web. They used to visit a specific site to complete a task. For example, if they wanted the latest news about a specific crisis, they went directly to CNN or the BBC. But more recently, they're looking to search engines. The search engine takes the user directly to the information they require, bypassing the site's home page. This deep linking seriously reduces the home page's prominence.

Google Reader is just one of many RSS readers that let users view new content from multiple websites at the same time, bypassing website home pages.

Another factor in the decline of home pages is the rise of RSS feeds. RSS gathers content from multiple websites in a RSS reader. Users no longer have to check sites for updated content, because that content comes to them. This push-oriented approach is great because it doesn't rely on users checking your site. But it does diminish the number of visits to your home page, because the RSS feed either contains your content or links deep within your website.

These two factors have shifted the focus of websites away from home pages and toward content. The home page is still important, but it isn't as important as it once was. If you're struggling to convince people about the home page's decline, the next technique is to delay its design.

Rushing into home-page design

Much of the conflict surrounding the home page focuses on what content it should include, rather than on its design. By starting with something less controversial, such as a text page, you can set the design for the site before the fight for real estate dilutes it.

A home page should reflect the content of a site at the highest level and signpost key content deeper in the site. In many projects, the content hasn't been finalized at the initial design stage. It's hard to create an effective home page without a full understanding of what content should be signposted. It's better to leave the home page alone until you have a clearer understanding of the site's content. When you finally address the home page, be sure to demonstrate the importance of simplicity to your stakeholders.

Demonstrating the importance of simplicity

Simplicity is important. As the website owner, you must fully embrace this idea. And you must communicate it effectively to the project's stakeholders. In the context of your home page, design simplicity equates to a single principle: *The more elements you add to your home page, the less importance each has.*

John Maeda sums it up beautifully in his book *The Laws of Simplicity (Simplicity: Design, Technology, Business, Life)* (MIT, 2006). He says, "The opportunity lost by increasing the amount of blank space is gained back with enhanced attention on what remains."

Compare these two well-known search engines. Which better communicates its primary function? Which is more intuitive to use? Is it any wonder Google dominates search?

To help both yourself and your stakeholders grasp the power of simplicity, I recommend the following exercise:

1. *Write a list of all the elements that need to appear on your home page.* Some items will be interface elements, such as navigation or search. Others will be brand related, such as the logo. Still others will be content related, such as a latest-news box or a list of quick links. The latter will probably be the longest list, because different stakeholders will push their own agendas. But always remember that the website should be less about what internal stakeholders want and more about the needs of users. Ask yourself, "What matters to users when they first arrive on our home page?"

2. *When the list is complete, assign yourself 15 points.* Each point represents a small amount of attention the user will give your home page. The underlying principle is that a user has a finite amount of attention.

3. *Begin assigning points to elements from your list.* Any element that appears on a page must be assigned at least one point. The more points you assign it, the more attention it will be given. This approach demonstrates that the more you add to a page, the more likely it is that important elements will get lost in the crowd.

Carry out this exercise with your stakeholders and (when possible) designers. It will help clarify what is important and bring some structure to the development of your home page. Although this exercise is effective at resolving content and prioritization, it doesn't help with aesthetics such as branding.

CORPORATE BRANDING

Brand identity varies from one organization to the next. In some businesses, all that exists is an ill-defined logo, which is regularly altered to suit the whim of the designer. Elsewhere, a weighty document specifies every aspect of the brand identity, including the use of color, imagery, typography, and logo. Whether your corporate guidelines are excessive or non-existent, it can be challenging to bring a brand online.

Branding guidelines range from extensive to nothing at all. Both extremes present problems.

Creating a personality for your brand

Designers need clearly established brand guidelines to produce an appropriate design. If that brand doesn't exist or is poorly defined, your designer will be forced to develop it. The website owner must work with them.

It's unnecessary to produce a full corporate style guide. All you need is an idea of how the site should feel. Ask yourself what type of personality your brand has. If the brand were a person, what type of person would it be? Would it be friendly or formal, carefree or conservative, professional or personable? How old and what gender would it be? What car would it drive, and what newspaper would it read? Assigning your brand personality gives the designer direction when selecting color, typography, and layout.

Find your brand's personality

Look to offline material for inspiration about your brand. The colors, text, and design of this Lynx shower bottle say a lot about the personality of the brand. Lynx is obviously young, male, and obsessed with girls. The company's website (http://lynxeffect.com) reflects this perfectly.

How do you go about establishing your brand's personality? Look at existing marketing and sales collateral. Are the colors somber and conservative? What about the copy—is it written in the first or third person? Is it conversational or formal? How does the company project itself to the outside world? Look at the company's business objectives, and speak to internal stakeholders about how they perceive the personality of the company. Establish a plumb line against which design decisions can be made.

In addition, you can use existing sales and marketing material more literally in determining the design of your web project. It can guide the look in terms of color, typography, imagery, and layout. But sticking to offline material too closely can cause problems.

Going from print to the web

The problem with using existing marketing material as a guide for your web project is that it's usually print based. Also, most style guides are produced by traditional advertising agencies, many of whom have little or no experience developing for the web. These guidelines often make no reference to the web and don't always conform to best practice.

But a style guide can be valuable if you treat its contents as guidelines rather than unbreakable rules. A degree of flexibility is required to make the transition to the web. Three areas can prove particularly problematic:

> Logo design

> Corporate fonts

> Color

Let's start with logo design.

Logo design

Brand guidelines focus heavily on logo usage. Specifications are supplied for size, color, position, background, and whitespace. But sometimes, these rules can't be applied to the web. For example, when monitor size varies and screen resolutions can be set by users, defining measurements in millimeters and centimeters is useless.

On other occasions, it would be unwise to follow guidelines. This typically happens with specifications about the position of a logo. On the web, the convention is that your logo is placed at upper left. Positioning the logo elsewhere makes it harder for users to identify the site and conflicts with their expectations. It's better to ignore guidelines in such situations and instead stick with web conventions.

Because a computer screen can display less information than print, logos and type often appear pixilated at smaller sizes. This problem can be so acute that it affects legibility.

A more serious problem is the logo itself. One of the most significant differences between the web and print is *dots per inch* (dpi). This term originated in print design. It refers to the detail at which a page is printed. A printed page is made up of a series of dots; the more dots in a single inch, the more detailed and crisp the printed material appears. The same principle is used on the web; but instead of printed dots, there are pixels. Most logos are printed at between 300 and 600 dpi, but on the web they're rarely displayed higher than 72 dpi. This difference in quality means logos can appear pixilated and lack detail at smaller sizes.

Most of the time, this difference in resolution isn't a problem. But when a logo is particularly complex, it can become illegible when shown at a smaller size. In such situations, the designer is left with two options: increase the size of the logo, taking valuable real estate away from content; or consider a web version of the logo, which is simplified to support the lower resolution.

Dpi can also be a problem with corporate typefaces.

Corporate fonts

Typography is an important part of your brand identity, but it can be problematic on the web. Ornate and serif typefaces can render poorly, becoming illegible at smaller sizes.

Poor rendering isn't the only problem with web typography. To display a font, users must have it installed on their PC, limiting the choice of fonts a designer has available. Furthermore, the web designer can only safely use fonts that come with the operating system. Because not all PCs run the same operating system, this limits you to about nine typefaces.

Although this sounds depressing, things aren't as bad as they first appear. For a start, it's possible to create a hierarchy of fonts. In other words, the designer can specify a primary font

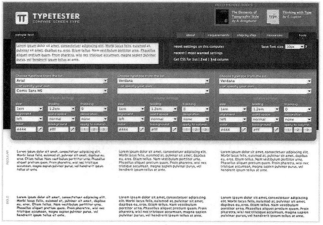

Typetester (http://www.typetester.org/) compares different web-safe typefaces and displays all the default fonts available on different operating systems.

The new Headscape site (unlike the old site shown in chapter 2) uses images to display headings in the corporate font. It uses Helvetica for body copy and falls back on Arial if Helvetica isn't available.

and, if that isn't available, fall back on safer fonts. This approach has some drawbacks but generally is reliable.

It's also possible to use custom fonts in Adobe Flash or images. But designers use this approach sparingly (normally only for headings) because it can create accessibility problems, confuse search engines, and increase download time.

There is hope for the future. For some time, it has been theoretically possible to use custom fonts that are downloaded along with the web page. This would allow a website to use any font, without it being installed. Unfortunately, until recently, none of the major browsers have supported this functionality. But the situation is beginning to change: support exists in Safari, Firefox, and Opera. Unfortunately, at the time of writing, Internet Explorer hasn't followed suit.

For now, the best you can expect is to use corporate fonts for headings, with the majority of typography being rendered in one of the web-safe fonts. Speaking of web safe, let's look at the much-misunderstood area of color on the web.

Color

There was a time when designers had to work with web-safe colors. Some people suffer from the misconception that this is still the case. Thankfully, the vast majority of personal computers can now render millions of colors perfectly well.

That said, colors on the web don't display the same as in print. In print, color is produced through the application of ink on paper. On the web, mixing red, green, and blue light creates the colors you see. Different monitors, computers, and operating systems all display color slightly differently. These differences mean it isn't enough to take the Pantone numbers found in most style guides and apply them to the web.

The problem becomes particularly acute when corporate palettes contain light or dark colors. Because of the way colors are shown on screen, light colors become lighter and dark colors get darker. On some screens, dark colors can appear almost black, whereas a light color can appear almost white.

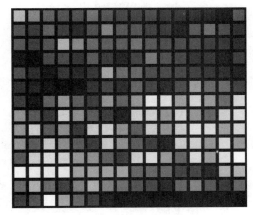

Once, web designers were limited to only 216 colors. Thankfully, that is no longer the case.

Ultimately, the designer has to solve this problem. Keeping in mind that colors vary from monitor to monitor, try viewing designs on as many different computers as possible before you comment on the color. What looks great on your laptop may appear too dark or too light on your colleague's old home monitor.

It's easy to forget just how different the web is from print. But those differences aren't confined to style guides. They apply to layout as well.

THE CHALLENGES OF LAYOUT

Creating an effective layout for a website is a skill. A good designer can lead the user's eye around a page, drawing attention to key elements by using size, position, and color. Designers use techniques such as whitespace, grid systems, and web conventions to make a design easy to understand. Understanding how layout on the web works defines a good designer.

It's beyond the scope of this book to teach you the principles of good layout, because you don't need to know them. You can assess the effectiveness of a layout by carrying out design or usability testing (usability testing is covered in chapter 6).

What you *do* need to know are three underlying concepts that dictate layout on the web:

> Screen resolution

> The fold

> Page width

We'll start with screen resolution because it directly affects the other two.

The GetFirefox website does an excellent job of using color, position, and size to draw the user's attention to the large Download button.

Grappling with resolution

Screen *resolution* refers to the number of pixels displayed on screen at any one time. Some computers can display 800 pixels across the width of the screen and 600 pixels in height. Others may be set at 1,024 pixels wide and 768 pixels high. The more pixels, the smaller each pixel is.

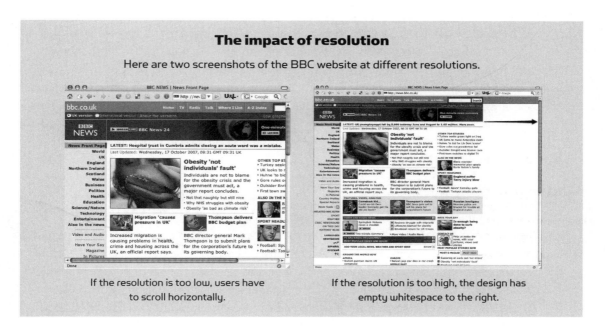

The impact of resolution

Here are two screenshots of the BBC website at different resolutions.

If the resolution is too low, users have to scroll horizontally.

If the resolution is too high, the design has empty whitespace to the right.

The user can manually alter the number of pixels being displayed. People often choose to do so to make screen elements appear bigger or smaller. If someone has poor vision, icons and text may appear too small at higher resolutions. By lowering the resolution, everything looks proportionally bigger because each individual pixel is larger. Conversely, some people want more space on their desktop, so they increase the resolution. Each pixel is reduced in size, so everything looks smaller and sharper.

Screen resolution affects web design in two ways. First, if a website is built to a fixed width (let's say 780 pixels), it will almost fill the screen at a lower resolution like 800 x 600. But at a higher resolution like 1,024 x 768, empty space will appear around it. As the resolution increases even more, the site will begin to look very small. Of course, the opposite is also true. If you build your website at a larger size, then at a lower resolution you'll get horizontal scrollbars. Horizontal scrolling has been proven in user testing to be one of the worst hazards to usability.

Problems with resolution also affect legibility. If a user is running at a high resolution, everything appears smaller, and this can cause difficulties when reading small text. In theory, the user could lower their resolution to make everything more legible, but that rarely happens. This is partly because users don't want to continually adjust their resolution based on each site they visit. But mainly, most users don't know how to change the resolution.

What is the solution to the problem of resolution? The answer lies in something we've already discussed: web statistics. Tools like Google Analytics can tell you what screen resolution your visitors are using. This should help you determine the width and font sizes of your site. Be careful: it's easy to dismiss the 10% of your users who are running at 800 x 600 when 90% are running at 1,024 x 768 or higher. Horizontal scrolling is such a usability handicap that you're effectively turning away 10% of your audience. Can you afford to do that?

Resolution affect not only horizontal scrolling but also vertical scrolling and the point known as the *fold*.

Understanding the fold

This idea references the fold in newspapers when they're placed on a newsstand. Because people passing by see only the top half of the front page, it became important for the lead story to appear "above the fold" to catch people's attention.

The idea has been transplanted to the web and refers to the point at which people have to begin scrolling. Much as with newspapers, the idea is that important content is placed above the fold to hook people and draw them in. Some believe that users are so bad at scrolling that all content should be kept above the fold, especially on the home page.

Earlier in this chapter, we looked at three techniques for improving home page sign-off. I believe there is a fourth: accepting that *the fold is a myth*. Too many people exacerbate the problems of content overload by insisting that all content sit above this mythical line.

The fold doesn't exist. In the newspaper industry, you can clearly define where the fold falls. On the web, any number of factors affect the point where users begin to scroll:

> *Resolution*—Screen resolution affects the vertical space available and so affects the position of the fold.

> *Browser*—Different browsers use different amounts of space at the top of the page for buttons, bookmarks, and the address bar.

> *Toolbars*—Most browsers let you turn on and off various toolbars as well as install new ones. From the Google toolbar to social-networking features, it's possible to have several toolbars showing at once.

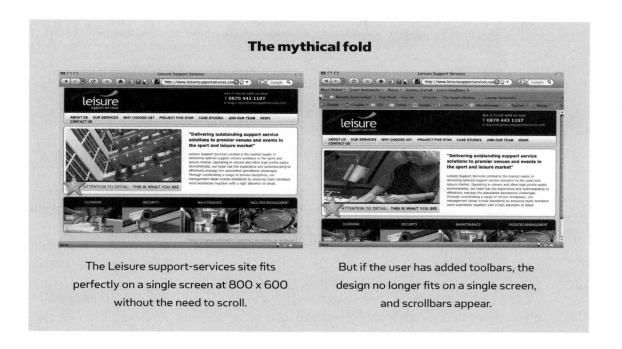

The Leisure support-services site fits perfectly on a single screen at 800 x 600 without the need to scroll.

But if the user has added toolbars, the design no longer fits on a single screen, and scrollbars appear.

What about the perception that users don't scroll? Some of the early research by usability expert Jakob Nielsen indicated that users didn't scroll. But as early as 1997, he wrote the following:

> *In more recent studies, we've seen that most users scroll when they visit a long home page or a long navigation screen. This change in behavior is probably due to users getting more experience with scrolling Web pages.*
> *… Scrolling is no longer a usability disaster for navigation pages. Scrolling still reduces usability, but all design involves trade-offs, and the argument against scrolling is no longer as strong as it used to be.*

This belief that users are becoming increasingly comfortable with scrolling has been further reinforced by ClickTale (http://www.clicktale.com/), a software company whose product monitors user behavior. Research carried out in 2006 showed that 76% of

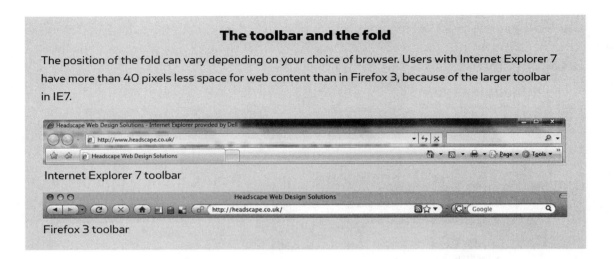

The toolbar and the fold

The position of the fold can vary depending on your choice of browser. Users with Internet Explorer 7 have more than 40 pixels less space for web content than in Firefox 3, because of the larger toolbar in IE7.

Internet Explorer 7 toolbar

Firefox 3 toolbar

pages with scrollbars were scrolled to some extent. This figure is probably even greater because it doesn't take into account users returning to a page. They don't need to scroll again because they already know what content is available.

The idea of a fold is unhelpful and undermines usability when attempts are made to fit as much content as possible above it. A better approach is to establish a clear visual information hierarchy regardless of an unknown scroll point.

The best approach is to ensure that you view any design concepts on as many different computers as possible. That will enable you to see what the design looks like at different resolutions, in different browsers, and with different toolbars.

The final area that can cause confusion concerning layout has to do with the various techniques used to constrain page width.

Constraining page width

You can use three basic approaches to set the width of web pages:

> *Fixed*—The site has a set pixel width. No matter what changes you make to the size of the browser window, the site doesn't change.

> *Fluid*—The site is designed to scale and fill the entire browser window. As the user alters the window size, the site adapts to fill the available space.

> *Elastic*—The site determines its width based on the text size defined in the browser settings. If the user enlarges the text, the width of the entire site increases.

It's often not clear from design mockups how the page will be constrained. Most design concepts are shown as image files rather than working web pages because it's quicker to mock up a design image than to build a functional web page. An image of a design is always fixed width, making it difficult to visualize how the site will work.

There is little you can do to overcome this problem. But you should discuss with the designer whether a design will be fixed width, fluid, or elastic whenever you receive a mockup.

Choosing between layout approaches can be a daunting task.

Description	Low resolution	High resolution

Fixed layout—At low resolutions, the design fills the screen. But at high resolutions, whitespace shows.

Fluid layout—The design fills the screen at both low and high resolutions, but long line lengths can be a problem.

Elastic layout—The design resizes as the user alters the text size, effectively zooming the design.

Which approach is best? At its heart, the argument comes down to control. Should the designer dictate how the site appears, or should the user be given control? A fixed-width design gives the designer pixel-perfect control. The design is entirely predictable, with images appearing in exact positions and content displayed at a particular line length. If your highest priority is branding and designs, then a fixed-width site is preferable. This is particularly true if the vast majority of your users are viewing at a certain resolution, and you can design for that.

A fluid design lets the user dictate (to some extent) how the design looks. Users can resize the browser window to suit their needs, and the design adapts accordingly. This is generally considered a more accessible approach because it supports a broader range of screen resolutions and lets the design adapt to individual user requirements. The downside is that you lose pixel-perfect control. The design won't look exactly as it did when mocked up, and it can take longer to build and test.

Elastic is in many ways a compromise. Although the design doesn't resize based on browser size, it does support users who want to increase the size of text. It maintains some of the design control of fixed but allows some of the flexibility of fluid. Of course, this means the design also inherits the negative elements of both. Elastic designs can suffer from horizontal scrolling like fixed and unpredictable layout like fluid.

As with all aspects of developing a design, the approach you choose should evolve from a discussion between you and the designer. For example, the designer may suggest a compromise in which a fluid design is constrained by a minimum and maximum width. These kinds of decisions need to be made on a per-project basis.

Next actions

In this chapter, we've looked at the challenges of design. We've addressed the divisive nature of design, including the difficulties of the home page and brand guidelines. We've also looked at the fold, screen resolutions, and page-constraint techniques. This discussion should help inform and smooth your design process. The designer should be able to propose design solutions.

But that isn't the end of the process. The designer now needs to roll out the design across the entire site. You can facilitate that process by completing three actions:

ACTION 1: *Define your content.* Before the designer can implement the new visual identify, they must know more about the content. Draw up a list of what the site should cover. What messages do you wish to communicate? What functionality are you going to provide?

ACTION 2: *Compile the design assets.* The designer needs any visual content that must appear on your site. This should include photography, illustrations, graphs, and video. If there are visuals you would like to include but don't have, speak to your designer about using a stock library for images or video. It may even be appropriate to commission photography or video for the site.

ACTION 3: *List the design templates.* After you have a feel for the content on your site, work with the designer to identify any areas that may need special design attention. The majority of pages will use standard text templates; but there are always special cases, such as search results or download pages, that need more consideration.

Identifying the content that you wish to include is only the tip of the iceberg. Next, you need to write and collate that content, as well as work with the web-design agency to structure it in a logical fashion.

5

Creating killer content

In this chapter

This is the first book I have written, and the process has involved a steep learning curve. What has struck me most is how much consideration I give to my writing here compared to the content I publish on my website. Even though more people read my blog than will read this book, I have spent considerably longer agonizing over what I say in these pages.

I'm not alone in this attitude. Only rarely have I come across a website owner with the budget to employee a professional copywriter or editor. It's unusual to find an organization willing to dedicate resources to rewriting content for the web. Instead, it's often acquired from other sources and dumped unceremoniously online.

In this chapter, I'll describe how to create killer content for your site and explain why it's so important to give your content the same attention it would receive if you were writing a book. I would even argue that writing well for the web is more challenging than writing a book.

LEARN THE IMPORTANCE OF CONTEXT

On larger websites, the role of managing content can become so demanding that it's sometimes assigned to a separate editor. But with so few organizations willing to pay for a web editor, the job often falls to the website owner. To effectively fill in for the role of website editor, you need to understand that on the web, *context* is king, not *content*.

The power of context isn't unique to the web. A billboard's ad copy has to be short and snappy. Drivers don't stop to read roadside advertisements.

The web has unique characteristics that affect what content you put online and the way that content is written. I'll focus on three of those characteristics:

> Reading from a screen

> The impact of the link

> Easy access to other sites

Each of these characteristics profoundly affects the way users interact with your site.

Don't make users read online

Although emerging technologies such as electronic paper give me hope for the future, screen legibility is currently extremely poor for two reasons. First, the majority of monitors display text at a considerably lower resolution than print. Second, instead of ink printed on paper, monitors project light; and over time, this can cause eye strain.

The result is that users rarely choose to read online for any length of time. You need to accommodate this characteristic in your copy. In short, you need to keep your copy concise.

Providing context through links

The power of the web lies in a simple invention: the humble hypertext link. The ability to link pages and for users to follow these links in any order dramatically alters the way you write content.

Although each page is part of a bigger whole, it also needs to stand alone. A user may have arrived on a specific page directly from a search engine, bypassing the rest of your content. Content must be written in a modular manner.

The link both creates and solves this problem. By adding links to related information in your copy, you can provide context where it's lacking. Linking also allows you to provide more detail without diluting the core message. In some ways, writing for the web is like writing newspaper headlines or billboard ads: you have to be short, snappy, and engaging, because users aren't going to hang around to read things thoroughly. Pages at the highest level needs to focus on communicating your core message. But an interested user will want more. Luckily, the web lets you link to pages deeper in the site and provide additional detail.

The danger with asking users to drill

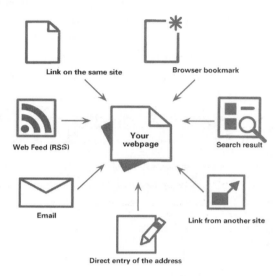

With users coming to a web page from any number of different sources, it's important that your content be understandable without context.

down for more detail is that it becomes hard to find the information they require. The key is to identify what users need and make sure it's accessible from the highest levels of the site. Later in this chapter, we'll explore ways of doing this through card sorting.

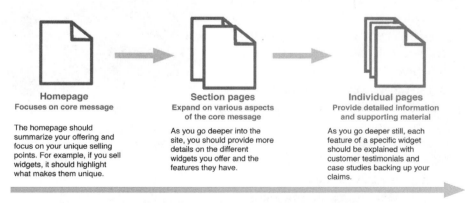

Homepage
Focuses on core message

The homepage should summarize your offering and focus on your unique selling points. For example, if you sell widgets, it should highlight what makes them unique.

Section pages
Expand on various aspects of the core message

As you go deeper into the site, you should provide more details on the different widgets you offer and the features they have.

Individual pages
Provide detailed information and supporting material

As you go deeper still, each feature of a specific widget should be explained with customer testimonials and case studies backing up your claims.

The deeper the user navigates into the site, the more detail becomes available.

Reducing the desire to leave

Web users will look elsewhere if they become frustrated. If information is hard to find, badly written, or full of jargon, it's easy to hit the back button and try another site. Copy has to be clear, concise, and engaging. It needs to be well organized, allowing users to easily access information. This will give your site an edge over your competition. Copy has to be concise for the context of the web. You need to look at the content on your site and ask yourself if it can be removed or reduced.

How context informs content

Understanding the context of the web determines how you write content in four ways:

- Because reading on the web is difficult, content needs to be concise.
- The hypertext link means you must carefully structure your content.
- With the competition a click away, copy must be engaging and informative.

Content must be written to work in isolation. Users many not have seen other pages on your site.

REDUCE OR REMOVE

In chapter 4, "Differences over design," you produced a list of content areas to include on your site to help brief the designer. This list is also the starting point for defining your site's final content.

The list you drew up is probably considerable. But although there is much you *could* add to your site, that doesn't mean you *should*. It's easy to put every available piece of information you have online.

In reality, you need to be ruthless, ascertaining whether each piece of content is really needed. The biggest part of creating website content is deciding what to leave out.

There is no shortage of sources from which you can draw content for your new site. The question is what to leave out.

Learning where to prune

You need to reduce content on two distinct levels. On a macro level, remove unnecessary pages and sections. On a micro level, assess each page and remove or reduce individual sentences or paragraphs.

In his book *The Elements of Style* (1979), E.B. White addresses the need to reduce your content on the micro level: "Vigorous writing is concise. A sentence should contain no unnecessary words, a paragraph no unnecessary sentence, for the same reason that a drawing should have no unnecessary lines and a machine no unnecessary parts."

In his book *Don't Make Me Think* (2006), Steve Krug suggests that you should "Get rid of half the words on each page, then get rid of half of what is left."

This harsh reduction in content must apply not only to individual paragraphs and sentences but also to the pages and sections. This approach provides tangible benefits:

> It reduces the chance of a user becoming lost.

> It makes useful content more prominent.

> It prevents users from becoming overwhelmed.

> It helps users find content more quickly.

The old adage of "less is more" is as true on the web as in any other part of life. After you accept the need to reduce content, the next issue becomes how to decide what to keep and what to reject.

Understanding how to prune

The best way to start pruning is to look at how easily information can be sourced. I worked with a charity that promoted the conservation of butterflies and moths. They had the great idea of building an application that helped users identify moths and butterflies.

Although they had the expertise necessary to identify species, the information was contained solely in people's heads. There was no database or identification book. With over 2,600 species of moths, it would have been prohibitively time consuming to

Writing content can be time consuming. If you need others to contribute, be sure they've been allocated time to do so.

get these experts to record their knowledge in a usable form. They had failed to consider the practicalities.

This is a common problem. It's easy to come up with great ideas for content, but it's much harder to source that content. Will the benefit of this content justify the effort involved in getting it onto the site?

Many web projects are delayed because key content needs to be generated by somebody who is too busy. Before committing to using a particular piece of content, ask yourself who will produce it, and ensure that they have the time. If they don't, work with that person and their manager to see if the website content can be prioritized.

Dismissing content because it's to hard to source probably won't reduce your content sufficiently. To reduce beyond that, you have to make a judgment call. How do you make that decision?

Where planning pays off

The best method of judging content's value is to refer to the background material you produced in chapter 2, "Stress-free planning." Business objectives, success criteria, and user personas not only inform the brief and the design process but also are instrumental in deciding what content should go on the site. I recommend a three-step approach to reducing content:

Step 1: Does the content help meet your business objectives?
For example, how does a page about company history help sell more widgets on your e-commerce site? If the answer is "it doesn't," then it shouldn't appear.

Step 2: Does the content contribute toward your success criteria?
If your goal is to increase inquiries by 25%, will a specific piece of content help or hinder that? If you include too much information on your site, users may not feel the need to call with questions. But if you have too little information, they become frustrated.

Step 3: What would your user personas think of your content?
Will your users read the content? Will it help them complete their goals? If not, remove it.

Cold, hard facts

Web logs are a useful way of gauging how popular a piece of content is. If the content is already online and monitored by a tracking package such as Google Analytics, it's easy to view that content by popularity. You can look at how many people visited a particular page and how long they spent there. The latter is important because if the user visits a page and then immediately leaves, it's an indication that the content isn't of value.

Where statistical information isn't available, the best course of action is to put the content online for a trial period and monitor its popularity. If the page fails to perform, remove it. Continually evaluate the success of individual pages.

This techniques should help you trim down your content significantly, but how do you go that extra mile? How do you "half it again," as Steve Krug would say?

Google Analytics lets you view content sorted by either page views or time spent on the page. Both provide a valuable indication of a page's value to users.

From macro to micro

The key is to shift your focus from removing whole sections of content to editing at the micro level. Start by targeting two distinct types of content that creep into many websites: marketing blurbs and instructional text.

Marketing blurbs can be found far beyond the web and appear in all kinds of promotional material. Such copy is full of its own self importance and devoid of real information. Good promotional copy informs as well as sells. In contrast, marketing blurbs shout about how good the product or service is without providing tangible evidence to support the claim.

Marketing blurbs are also the "happy talk" (as Steve Krug puts it) that you find on many home pages. Copy like this does nothing to

Web copy should be more than a marketing blurb. It should be information-focused and provide details to back up any marketing claims.

answer users' questions or direct them toward achieving their goal. It's the written equivalent of small talk. Users also rarely read instructional text—they would prefer to muddle through rather than read instructions. Such copy is therefore often ignored.

Your aim should be to eliminate instructions entirely by making the site intuitive. Where you can't achieved this, you should reduce instructions to the fewest possible words.

In the process of identifying and pruning your copy, you'll begin to think about how it should be organized and structured. After you've stripped out the dead wood, it's time to work on your site's information architecture.

USER-CENTRIC STRUCTURE

Information architecture refers to the way content is organized. The most common expression of this is the site map. A *site map* is the hierarchical structure of your site organized in a way similar to a family tree. Much of the terminology draws from this analogy. Each page has a *parent* (the page immediately above it in the site hierarchy). It may also have *children* (those pages below) and *siblings* (those on the same level).

Although there is much more to information architecture than the site map, this is the area in which you'll have most involvement. Working with the web designer or possibly an information architect, you must decide on a site structure. Because the website owner is often involved in the process of creating a site structure, it's important that you understand the basic techniques and common mistakes involved in its creation. One such technique is known as *card sorting*.

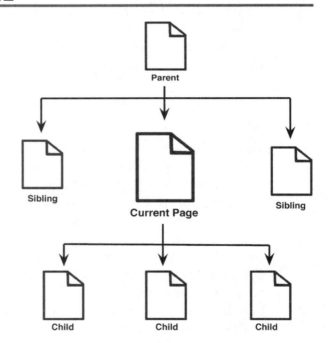

The terminology used to describe the levels of a site map is similar to that used on a family tree.

Structuring through card sorting

Card sorting is an effective way to begin structuring your website's content. Each individual area in your final content list is written on a separate card. These cards are then sorted into piles of related content, and each pile is named, thus creating a section.

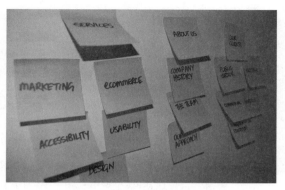

Often, the easiest approach is to pin these cards onto a wall and sort them from there. You can name each pile by attaching a post-it note to the top. By using cards and post-it notes, you can try different approaches and naming conventions until something works.

A variety of software packages have been designed to make it easier to create a site map. But there is something flexible and tactile about using post-it notes or index cards.

Card sorting is a powerful tool when web designer and owner work together, but it's even more useful when end users also participate. The most common use of card sorting is to understand users' mental models.

Carrying out a card-sorting exercise with end users requires a slightly different approach. The main difference is that you should significantly reduce the number of cards. Asking an end user to sort and organize several hundred cards is unrealistic in most circumstances. Approximately 30 cards is a more manageable number, unless you can spend considerable time working with each user. This means you'll need to do some initial sorting in advance.

You may also want to presort the cards into sections before the session begins. Users can find it hard to organize cards when working from a completely unsorted starting point. When given a structure to evaluate, they normally find the exercise much easier and quickly begin suggesting organizational structures of their own.

Such prestructuring will inevitably bias the results. This can cause a problem if you're taking a quantitative approach to the exercise. But allowing site structure to be dictated by numbers (for example, 86% of users placed this page under this section) rather than having a predefined structure is inappropriate. I recommend a qualitative rather than quantitative approach.

Using a qualitative approach, the person running the session questions the user about their decisions. Qualitative testing is much more interactive and less observational, allowing you to understand the specifics of how users organize the cards. The aim is to encourage the user to articulate their thoughts, thereby revealing their mental model. This lets you make informed decisions about the site's structure.

Although card sorting works well for informational sites made up of many separate pages, a growing number of web projects are more like web applications than multi-paged websites. In such cases, a site map isn't always adequate to explain the structure of the site, and you should create a use case.

Going with the flow

Producing a *use case* involves identifying a single goal that a user may have (for example, buying a product) and identifying the process they would take to achieve that goal. This can be recorded in written form or as a diagram. The use case should also note the exceptions that may occur in the process, as well as the main flow. Note where something goes wrong, such as when the user mistypes their credit-card number. Use cases help with more complex tasks like site registration, e-commerce transactions, and recovering lost passwords. The following is a use case for recovering a lost password:

> ### User-recovery process for a lost password
>
> Main scenario (when things go smoothly):
> 1. User provides email address.
> 2. System verifies email and retrieves password.
> 3. System sends email to the specified email address.
>
> Exceptions (when things go wrong):
> - No email is entered
>   - ☒ *The user is asked to enter an email address.*
> - The email address is incorrectly formatted
>   - ☒ *The user is asked to correct their email address.*
> - The email address isn't found
>   - ☒ *The user is told that the address can't be found and is asked to try again or register.*

The example involves a number of exceptions. Each one requires that additional code and copy be written. Without the use case, a developer may not grasp the extent of the work, and you may be unaware of the additional copy required. It can be easy to miss these different eventualities.

Use cases and card sorting are only the tip of the information-architecture iceberg. To avoid making mistakes in this complex area, you must also know the common pitfalls.

Common mistakes in structuring sites

I see people make numerous mistakes when creating a structure for their sites, but two happen more than others. The first of these is in the naming of pages and sections.

Confusing naming

Let's look at a menu bar from a fictional company:

The first problem is jargon. Never assume your users know all the acronyms. They may be new to the sector or use a slightly different variation of your company's terminology. The names of your sections and pages should be free of jargon and potentially unfamiliar product names. Titles should be descriptive and use the plainest language possible.

In the example, Acme Elite is a site-mapping tool aimed at web developers. Because it's a new product, people may not have heard of it, so it should be described in clear language. And not everybody will know that CMS stands for *content management system*. The revised menu looks like this:

There is still more you can do. Although naming should be descriptive, it should also be short. Ideally, all menu items should be one or two words long. Users should be able to quickly scan a menu and identify the sections most likely to have content they need.

"Acme case studies & testimonials" is an obvious candidate for shortening. You can even go a step further. The constant reference to Acme is unnecessary and makes scanning more difficult. Users know what site they're on and don't need reminding. These small changes dramatically improve the menu:

Search-engine voodoo

Some sites repeat the company name in the menu because doing so is supposed to aid search-engine placement. Although it's possible that this may have a *small* effect, the drawbacks to usability are significant enough to undermine any benefits.

The final issue to highlight is inconsistent naming between what is shown on the menu bar ("About us") and the associated page title below ("Our team"). Be careful that the way you refer to pages doesn't change. Every link to a page should be referred to the same way.

Where a page title needs to be longer than the wording used in the menu item, be sure they mirror each other. Inconsistent naming can cause confusion, making users unsure whether they have previously viewed a page.

The final menu looks like this:

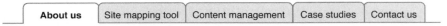

| About us | Site mapping tool | Content management | Case studies | Contact us |

About us

The second common pitfall is that of presenting the user with too many options.

Overwhelming options

I commonly come across site structures that include excessive links in the navigation. This is unwise because users may feel overwhelmed by too many options.

The desire to present many options is understandable. Website owners are pressured to ensure that certain content isn't buried deep within the site. There is also a misconception (often known as the *three-click rule*) that a user should be able to reach any page of your site in only three clicks.

Until recently, the Hartnell College home page overwhelmed users with too many options. Fortunately, it has remedied the problem.

Like many of the misconceptions relating to the web, the belief that users don't like to click is based on out-of-date thinking. The problem with clicks used to be the time a new page took to load. Today, that is less of a concern as broadband becomes more pervasive. Users don't mind additional clicks if they feel they're making progress.

This leaves the fear of content becoming buried. How will anybody discover a crucial product if it's four levels down? What if the user looks in the wrong section?

Remember that there is more to site navigation than the site's hierarchy. A good website provides numerous navigational tools to help the user find key content. These include:

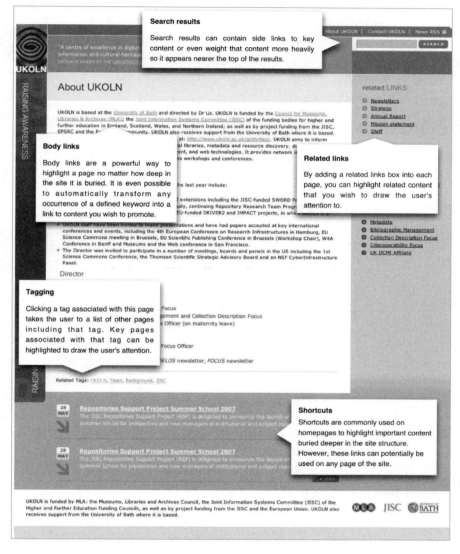

The traditional navigation bar isn't the only way users can find content. Many navigational tools are available.

Understanding the various navigational tools alongside the other techniques I've outlined should let you complete a site map for your site. The emphasis now shifts to editing your content and ensuring that it's engaging and easy to read.

SCANNABLE AND APPROACHABLE

It isn't within the scope of this book to equip you to be a copywriter; I assume you have some skill in that area or are adapting existing copy for the web. Instead, my focus is on techniques that can make copy more web friendly. These adaptations accommodate the unique medium through which you're communicating. These techniques can be reduced to three simple rules:

> Make it engaging.

> Make it clear.

> Make it scannable.

Let's begin with the need to make copy engaging.

Making your content engaging

From greeting you in German to using approachable terms and conditions, Flickr.com is an excellent example of a website that adds personality to its copy.

Computers and, by association, websites, are impersonal. At best, people perceive them as indifferent; at worst, they view them as hostile. It's important to counteract this perception.

The copy on your website should use a personal tone, written directly to the reader, and in the first person. It should be more informal than you would use if writing for a printed publication. This overcomes the coldness associated with computer interactions.

In chapter 4, "Differences over design," I suggested that you should consider the personality of your brand. If your brand was a person, how would that person speak? Would they be to the point or chatty? Friendly or formal? You need to reflect this personality in your writing.

Making it clear

The copy on your site needs more than personality. It must also be clearly written. Long sentences, complex punctuation, and uncommon words can be problematic.

Even if your target audience is well educated and has a high reading level, it's still good practice to avoid such pitfalls. Clear copy can be read and understood much more quickly. It's also more accessible to those with cognitive disabilities such as dyslexia. Most of all, it's easier to scan—and scanning is the key to successful online copywriting.

Making it scannable

The sad reality is that almost nobody will read your carefully crafted copy. Users rarely read a page online—rather, they scan it, looking for information or a link that will take them closer to their goal. If they come across a large block of text, they will probably ignore it, preferring to follow a link in the hopes of finding something more obviously useful.

> According to usability expert Jakob Nielsen, in 1997, only 16% of people read web pages word for word. Information overload has increased dramatically over the last decade, so that figure has almost certainly fallen sharply.

If you want to help users find the information they require and ensure that they read key messages, then you need to support scanning. Fortunately, you can do so using two simple techniques: front loading and breaking up blocks of text.

Be up front

Front loading is a technique that accommodates the way people scan a page. When a user comes across a new page, they're likely to read the first few lines of the first paragraph. If the content seems relevant, they scan the remainder of the page, reading the first few words of each paragraph until they find the content they're after.

Accommodate this habit in your writing. The first paragraph of the page should provide a summary of every-

Jakob Nielsen adds a summary to each article on his site so that people can quickly decide if it's relevant to them.

thing that follows, allowing the user to quickly ascertain if the page is relevant. Each paragraph should make its main point in the first sentence so that users can easily pick out relevant content.

Although this can be a tricky technique to master, it's worth the effort. Always have a summary of each page at the top of the main content area.

Break down the blocks

The second technique is to break large blocks of text into more manageable sections that can be scanned. You can break up content a number of ways, as demonstrated in the figure at below.

> **Headings** and subheadings allow users to find out if content is relevant without reading the main copy.

Get the right people in the right jobs

Our clients tell us that they are always on the hunt for new talent.

By 'tal
to chie
expert
level.

> **Highlight important content.** Whether you use bold and italic or do magazine-style pull-out quotes make sure important content stand out.

The c

There's no way round it; recruiting is an expensive process. Factor in advertising, interviews and assessment centres and 'ramp up' time and the cost can average over £9000 per new hire. Add headhunter fees into the equation and the cost to the business spirals into orbit...

Now imagine that a proportion of these hires turn out to be unsuitable for their new role. They may underperform or they might even leave. And the time and cost investment begins all over again...

Meanwhile the business does not have the full compliment of expertise it needs to achieve its objectives.

How can HR break this cycl

> **Keep paragraphs short.** Each paragraph should only communicate a single point.

The Getfeedback approach – manag   about clarity:

→ What exactly are you looking for?
→ How will you be sure that you've found it?

The science of understanding these two elements is advancing rapidly. We can now profile a role very accurately and measure an individual against this. This serves two purposes: it provides a filter through which to pass candidates and enables the business to manage the risk once they have recruited candidates. The information gathered at assessment stage can be carried forward when the hire joins the business. Everyone knows what they are getting and how to get the best out of the new resource.

Here's how:

> **Using bullet lists** instead of paragraphs of text where possible. Bulleted lists are easier to scan and reduce word count.

→ Accurately map the 'talent geograph
   profiles, competency frameworks
→ Seal the credibility of the selection pro
   business managers are involved - both
→ Minimise risk by creating an assessment process which profiles the 'whole person': technical competence, behavioural competence, personality, aptitude, motivation and cultural fit

⤷ Let's get specific. <u>Selection solutions.</u>

Each technique is designed to help users find relevant content on the page without reading every word.

By using these techniques in conjunction with everything else in this chapter, you should be able to create copy that is concise, user-centric, and scannable. In short, you'll be able to create killer copy.

Next actions

In this chapter, we've focused on the identifying, organizing. and editing written copy. But copy isn't the only type of content on your website. Three other types of content are worth noting:

- *Graphics*—A picture is worth a thousand words, and well-chosen imagery can replace paragraphs of text and aid scannability. From charts and graphs to photography and illustrations, graphics are vital components of a site's content.

- *Multimedia*—With the growth of broadband, we're seeing an explosion in multimedia content including video, animation, and audio. This can greatly enhance written content and aid comprehension, especially when you're trying to explain complex ideas or demonstrate unfamiliar products.

- *Applications*—Many websites are more than brochureware and contain almost desktop-like functionality. Driven by complex coding and extensive databases of information, these applications often provide killer content.

It's your responsibility to oversee the content in these areas. Before we move on, you need to repeat the steps from this chapter and apply them to these new types of content:

ACTION 1: *Identify your content.* Work with your development team to ascertain what is achievable within your budget. Can graphics be sourced or produced? What content is better explained with multimedia? Do you have the data to power the applications you want? Do you have the time and expertise to build them?

ACTION 2: *Organize your content.* As you develop your site map, take into account graphical and multimedia elements. Most of all, create use cases so that everybody knows how the application-based content will operate.

ACTION 3: *Edit your content.* Your graphics, multimedia, and applications should be easy to understand, clearly represented, and engaging, just like your copy. Work with your team to ensure that these principles are applied to all content.

The best way to tell if your content is effective is to test it on real users, which you'll do in the next chapter.

6

User-centric design

In this chapter

T hroughout the first five chapters of this book, I've mentioned the importance of usability. Whether I've been discussing the pillars of web design in chapter 1 ("The secret of a successful website") or creating site structures in chapter 5 ("Creating killer content"), the emphasis has been on supporting users through user testing.

Beyond design testing in chapter 4 ("Differences over design"), I haven't discussed the practicalities of *how* to perform user testing. In this chapter, I will. I'll present a strong business case for usability testing and dispel the myths that it's time-consuming and expensive. I'll also provide practical tips for running a user test session and how to interpret the results. Finally, we'll look at common usability mistakes and how best to avoid them.

It will fall to you as website owner to ensure that usability lies at the heart of everything you build online. Having a firm understanding of its importance and the techniques for implementing it is fundamental to the role.

Let's begin by looking at the benefits and perceived costs of usability testing.

THE PROFIT AND LOSS OF USABILITY

The subject of usability generates a dichotomy between what you think and what you do. You know it's good to focus on usability. You need only look at Apple and the iPod to know that it provides tangible benefits. But it's hard to prioritize usability when deadlines are looming and budgets are tight, so user testing gets pushed to the bottom of the agenda. It's as if the perceived losses of testing outweigh the potential profit. Are these assumptions true? Is user testing time-consuming and expensive?

Understanding perceived losses from user testing

A widespread perception exists that user testing is costly and time-consuming—to some extent, with good reason.

Traditional usability testing is expensive because it involves consultants, usability labs, and carefully selected users.

Traditionally, user testing cost millions and took weeks to complete. It was done in expensive usability labs with two-way mirrors, computer suites, and video surveillance. Large numbers of test subjects were required, to provide statistically relevant data. Each had to conform to a specific demographic profile, so recruitment was difficult. A usability consultant testing in a lab with carefully selected subjects is effective, but this approach is beyond the budgets and time frames of most organizations.

User testing doesn't need to be like this. It can be lightweight and inexpensive. You can also do it yourself. Although doing the testing yourself isn't the most effective approach, it's better than no testing at all. But even the most lightweight user testing requires some time and budget. Do the benefits outweigh this cost?

Understanding the real profit of user testing

The benefits provided by user testing can't be overstated. Even the most lightweight approach will have a profound affect on your web presence. The benefits of user testing include

> Quick detection of problems

> Increased user satisfaction

> Reduced support costs

> Increased efficiency

Let's look at each in turn.

Quick detection of problems

If you do user testing throughout your project, potential problems will be identified more quickly. Regular testing will also find technical bugs. If you can identify problems early, they're much easier to fix. The further you are into a project, the more expensive and time-consuming changes become.

User testing can uncover technical problems as well as usability issues.

Increased user satisfaction

Users who become frustrated with your site rarely return. They will never see the improvements you make or recommend your site to a friend. They may even criticize it. In the competitive world of the web, repeat visitors and customer recommendations are crucial.

Reduced support costs

Even if you have no competition or have a captive audience, you can't ignore usability. Poor usability generates large numbers of support calls and complaints. It's often more economical to user-test than to deal with extra support calls.

Increased efficiency

Finally, an easy-to-use site can provide monetary benefits through efficiency. This is most easily seen on intranets. An easy-to-use intranet allows users to complete tasks more quickly—and time is money.

To a lesser extent, this principle also applies to your public site. If users can complete tasks quickly, they will perceive your site as a time saver and visit regularly.

User testing can provide real return on investment. But you can realize this return only if you can keep the cost of user testing to a minimum. How do you do this?

BARGAIN-BASEMENT USABILITY

The bargain-basement approach to usability testing was pioneered by usability experts Steve Krug and Jakob Nielsen. Although they differ on the details, they agree on three key principles:

> Test a little but often.

> Use a limited number of testers.

> Don't become too concerned with who you test.

> These principles are crucial if you want to user-test while delivering on time and within budget. Let's look at each in turn.

Testing a little but often

Key to this approach is the principle of "little but often." Testing should occur throughout a web project's life cycle, and that means keeping testing lightweight.

Steve Krug calls this approach *cubicle testing*, where any new development is shown to colleagues to see if they can make sense of it. This simple form of testing is remarkably effective.

If you choose to be more sophisticated about who and how you test, never let that be at the expense of quantity.

Why "often" matters

When they're initially testing, many users get stuck at the first hurdle. A second round lets you fix those problems, allowing users to progress further and uncover new issues. The number of rounds is largely dictated by budget and time. But the more rounds, the more issues you'll uncover. This is true even with a limited number of testers.

Common usability mistakes

Jakob Nielsen annually updates his list of the 10 most egregious offenses against users on his website, http://useit.com/alertbox/9605.html.

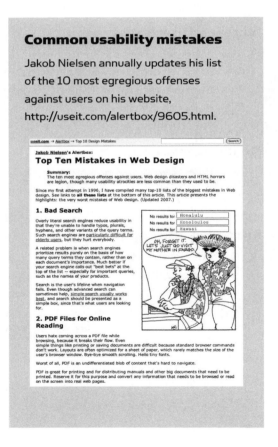

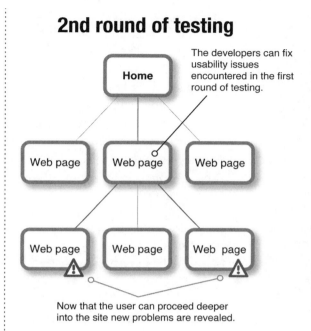

1st round of testing

Home

The user encounters a usability problem that prevents them continuing.

Web page

Web page

Web page

Web page

Web page

Web page

2nd round of testing

The developers can fix usability issues encountered in the first round of testing.

Home

Web page

Web page

Web page

Web page

Web page

Web page

Now that the user can proceed deeper into the site new problems are revealed.

The more rounds of testing, the more issues will be uncovered.

When should you schedule these numerous rounds?

When to test?

Before the project commences, *test your existing site or that of your competition*. These sites act as free prototypes that help identify potential usability issues. Next, *test sketches and design concepts*. Your designer may resist showing users unfinished work, but this is a valuable chance to identify issues before too much time has been invested.

When you're testing a design for usability, focus on whether the user gets it. Do they understand what the site is about and how it works? Does the user understand the terminology used. and are they paying attention to the right screen elements?

Before you begin production, *consider testing against a wireframe*. A *wireframe* is a disposable version of your site that contains cut-down design, content, and interaction. It provides a realistic experience against which to test. It's ideal for testing navigation and basic task completion.

The downside is that even a disposable wireframe can feel time-consuming and expensive to produce. But that is preferable to testing against a finished site, which can't easily be changed.

A number of tools can reduce the time spent building wireframes. The best time saver is to use a content management system (CMS) to construct your wireframe. If you do this well, you can reuse the CMS-driven wireframe as the basis of your final site. The wireframe is therefore no longer wasted.

User testing shouldn't end with the wireframe. As you build the site, test it. It's possible to test a half-finished site: select tasks for users to complete that focus on completed sections.

Wireframe tools

Omnigraffle is just one of the tools you can use to create wireframes. You can also use Visio, Powerpoint, or plain old HTML. There are also online tools such as jumpchart.com that help make the process easier.

Finally, *do a round of testing prelaunch*. By this stage, the majority of issues will have been discovered. But a last check will uncover minor problems that you can correct.

There are many opportunities for gathering user feedback, but you don't need to test at every stage. I recommend that *user testing should be an ongoing exercise even after launch*. Always seek new ways to make your site easier to use.

Now that you know *when* to test, the question becomes *who* to test.

Watching out for decreasing returns

Many website owners believe that usability testing is worthless if they don't test a large group of people within the target demographic. They're therefore discouraged from testing. But this belief isn't true.

Statistical testing as outlined earlier *is* expensive and time consuming. It doesn't provide significant benefits over the bargain-basement approach. In 2000, Jakob Nielsen (http://www.useit.com/alertbox/20000319.html) wrote, "Elaborate usability tests are a waste of resources. The best results come from testing no more than 5 users

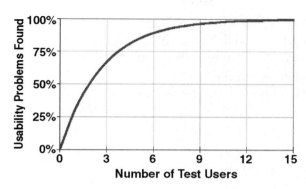

In his article "Why You Only Need to Test With 5 Users" (http://useit.com/alertbox/20000319.html), Jakob Nielsen demonstrates the diminishing returns that come from increasing the number of test subjects.

and running as many small tests as you can afford."

The reason is that the majority of users encounter the same problems when testing. The more users Nielsen tested, the more overlap he discovered in problems found by users. Eventually, the level of overlap is so high that the likelihood of discovering more issues is remote. As I said earlier, and as Nielsen reinforces, multiple rounds of testing are more effective.

Steve Krug takes the logic further, suggesting that you should test only three or four people. This catches the majority of serious issues, although admittedly some minor issues may slip through. Krug believes that this is a price worth paying, because testing three or four people lets you test and debrief in a single day.

In short, the more people you test, the lower your return on investment. This is also an issue for recruitment of testers.

Recruiting loosely

It's easy to waste time and money recruiting the perfect user who matches the personas you created earlier. This is fine if you have limitless resources. But it can't be allowed to reduce the number of rounds of testing.

Having the right users isn't as important as you may think. When testing usability (in preference to design or copy), most users encounter the same problems, no matter who they are. It's also good practice to design a site that is usable by all, not just by your exact target audience. That said, there are exceptions. It's unwise to test with users who have radically different levels of experience with the web. You should also be aware of any accessibility needs that may affect how your audience uses your site.

Being too specific about the demographics of your test subjects can make testing prohibitively expensive and time consuming.

A good example is a website aimed at the elderly. This audience has physical conditions that may affect their use of a site, and *generally* they don't have as much experience using the web as a younger demographic. You probably wouldn't want to test this site exclusively with 20-something technology geeks!

Now that you know who to recruit and in what numbers, you're almost ready to begin testing. But before you do, let's look at how to run an effective test session.

RUN AN EFFECTIVE TEST SESSION

Running your first usability session can be intimidating, especially if you've never even seen one. You probably have questions about where to run the session, what you're supposed to do, and what kind of things to cover.

Fortunately, running a test session is remarkably straightforward and can be done by almost anyone. You should follow these three simple principles:

> ➤ Be prepared.

> ➤ Understand the role of the facilitator.

> ➤ Work from a script.

How, then, do you prepare?

Do regular informal testing, too. Ask someone in the office who isn't involved with the project to look at your work.

Being prepared

It's possible to do usability testing with no preparation whatsoever, using the cubicle test mentioned earlier. But if you want to run something more formal, a little preparation goes a long way. Before you begin recruiting, answer two basic questions: where and when are you going to test?

If you can easily visit your testers, then you may wish to test where they normally access the web. This provides two advantages. First, they're more relaxed in their own surroundings. Second, you're seeing them in their native environment, which is more realistic. But doing this isn't always practical. The alternative is to ask testers to come to a central location. This need not be anywhere sophisticated—it can even be your desk.

Usability testing can be lightweight.
All you need is a random stranger, a PC, and a notetaker.

The most important requirements for the test environment are that it's quiet and that the tester not be disturbed. Although a constantly ringing phone may be realistic, it doesn't aid successful user testing!

When you know where you're going to test, draw up a schedule. Try to schedule all your sessions on a single day. Each session should last a maximum of 40 minutes, because people struggle to concentrate for longer that than. Placing sessions an hour apart gives you an opportunity to make additional notes and prepare for the next session. It also allows time for users who have a lot to share or struggle with their tasks.

Always expect at least one person to drop out. Somebody will always be too busy or sick to attend. Have a backup available to step in at the last minute. Even if this is a colleague who isn't involved in the project, it's better than nothing.

You've established where and when. The next question is, who does the testing?

Understanding the role of facilitator

The person responsible for running a usability test session is known as the *facilitator*. Unless you're using an expert, this role will probably fall to you. But are you the best person to carry out the testing? Could you use someone else instead?

Who should facilitate user testing?

The problem is that you're close to the project. You understand how the site works and may be tempted to guide users in the right direction. You're emotionally invested in the project, and it's hard for you to remain impartial.

Good facilitators should always remain calm. They need to be patient and good listeners, capable of drawing opinions from others. Unfortunately, not everyone is capable of that. I make a terrible facilitator—I talk far too much and get frustrated when users fail to get it. Ask yourself, are you the right person for the job? And if not, who is?

The facilitator's responsibilities

Whoever your facilitator is, they need to understand the role. The position has three responsibilities:

A facilitator should always be calm, patient, and a good listener.

> *To encourage the tester to communicate*—Many users sit in silence, struggling with a site, unless they're encouraged to speak. The facilitator should challenge users to think aloud. Ask open-ended questions that can't be answered with yes or no. Constantly ask what users are thinking, and question their choices.

> *To intervene when necessary*—There is a perception that the facilitator should never intervene to help a struggling tester. This idea is counterproductive. If a user becomes stuck, show them how to continue. This provides an opportunity to discuss why the way forward wasn't obvious and gives you a chance to discover other issues deeper in the site.

> *To lead the tester through the usability script*—It always pays to prepare a usability script beforehand that outlines what you intend to cover. It's the role of the facilitator to guide the tester through this script.

If a script is required, what should go into it? What should be tested and how?

Working from a script

What goes into a usability script largely depends on what you're testing. If it's a design concept, your testing will be limited to questions about the navigation and communication of core messages. You can also carry out some flash testing (as discussed in chapter 4); but beyond that, your options are limited.

Testing against a wireframe or early versions of the site allows users to complete key tasks. For example, you can ask users to find the price of a particular product or the contact details for a key staff member.

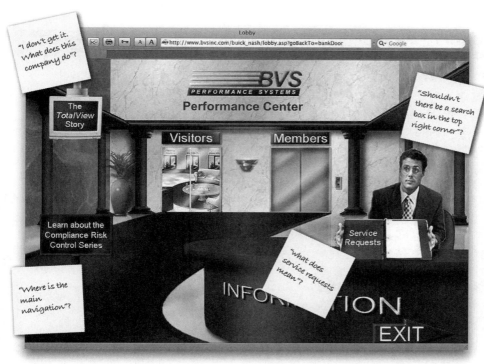

Basic testing on this site early on would have shown the approach was fundamentally flawed. The site has since been replaced.

Base the choice of a task on activities your personas would wish to complete. Think back to the persona you created in chapter 2. Jane is considering a visit to a health spa. You established that the first two pieces of information Jane wants are price and availability. Any user testing for the spa should include tasks to find this information.

Although what you test will vary depending on the project and stage of development, some information should always be included. The following are highlights from a fictional transcript demonstrating the information you should always cover:

Transcript excerpt	Explanation of the approach
Hi, Jane. My name is Paul, and I'm going to be running our session today. Joining me is Pete. I have asked him along to take some notes as we talk.	Introducing yourself and others in the room helps put the user at ease. Offering coffee helps, too! Be sure to explain any intimidating recording equipment.
We're here to improve a website that is under development. You're going to help us test the site. We are testing the site and *not* you, so you can relax!	By explaining to the user that you're testing the site and not them, you encourage them to behave more naturally.

Transcript excerpt	Explanation of the approach
You don't need to worry about messing up. There are no right or wrong answers in a usability test. What we do need is complete honesty. If you're struggling with something or don't like the way it works, say so. You aren't going to offend anybody.	If the user thinks the session is a test with right and wrong answers, they will tell you what they think is correct rather than what they feel. Many users are also worried about offending the facilitator. It's important to stress that you want honest answers and no offense will be taken.
The most important thing to remember is that we need you to explain what you're thinking. Think out loud, and talk about the options you're considering. Before you click a link, explain what other options you considered and why you picked that one.	Getting the user to articulate their thoughts is fundamental to the success of the session. This can't be stressed enough. Even though you explain the need up front, you'll still need to prompt the user throughout the session.
If you have any questions, feel free to ask. I may not be able to answer them right away, because I could prejudice the testing, but I'll answer them at the end.	It's important to explain before you begin why you may not answer questions during the session. If the user asks questions, be sure to address them at the end.
Let's start with something easy. Can you tell me a little about yourself? Tell me about your job.	Begin each session with simple questions such as family status, age, and job title. This helps build the user's confidence and provides some background information.
Tell me about your computer experience. How confident do you feel using a PC? Do you use a PC for work? At home? How much do you use the internet? What kind of sites do you use most and find useful?	Building up an understanding of the user's computer and web experience is useful context for the session. It also indicates how representative they are of the target audience.
Let's talk about the site. It's for a health spa. Before I show it to you, I want to ask about your expectations. What do you think a health spa website should look like, and what information should it contain?	It's often helpful to ask users about their expectations. If the expectations don't meet reality, it can cause confusion. This also it gives you the opportunity to find out more about what users want from the site.

After this introduction, the session becomes more specific. The direction depends on the material available to test against and the type of site. This specific testing should fall into the category of either "do they understand what they're seeing?" or task completion. When the testing is complete, the next challenge is how to respond to the results.

FIX THE PROBLEMS

Even after over a decade in web design, users still surprise me. They react unpredictably. What seems obvious to me mystifies them. Sitting through a usability session can be both frustrating and demoralizing.

User testing can feel overwhelming, especially the first time you do it. Many people go into usability testing hoping to validate the approach they have taken. Instead, it often does the opposite. Although things can appear to be a disaster, not every criticism requires a response, and not every problem needs fixing. The key is to filter and prioritize.

Filtering out background noise

The first step is to weed out distractions, starting with a design-related issue. During usability testing, participants often comment on aesthetics. This is a distraction for two reasons. First, the aim of usability testing isn't primarily to address visuals. Second, design is subjective, and comments like "I don't like the green" have little value. Unless you are specifically testing design or the vast majority of testers make the same comment, you can ignore anything said about design.

The second common distraction is suggestions for new content. Comments such as "Wouldn't it be good if the site did this?" don't

Filter out subjective opinion and suggestions that lead to scope creep.

help evaluate what is currently there. The scope of the project was defined much earlier in the process, and adding new content or functionality at this stage will lead to scope creep.

I'm not suggesting that ideas about content are worthless. As with design suggestions, if the vast majority of testers suggest something, you have to take their comments seriously. Ask whether you've missed something fundamental or whether it's a nice extra. If it's the latter, don't throw the suggestion away. Rather, add it to the list of ideas you compiled in chapter 2; these can be implemented in the future.

The final filter is return on investment. Sometimes a problem can't be fixed without investing a disproportionately large amount of money compared to the return received. In many cases, this is because of existing technology or business processes that can't be changed.

Although you can do things to minimize this inconvenience, you're ultimately limited by the realities of business.

Case study: Wiltshire Farm Foods

Wiltshire Farm Foods (http://www.wiltshirefarmfoods.co.uk/quickorder) is an e-commerce site that superbly demonstrates how business constraints sometimes need to come before usability considerations. Their site requires a postcode before displaying prices. During user testing, a number of participants made it clear that they were uncomfortable purchasing from a company that required personal data before showing prices.

There are good reasons for this approach. The company's entire business model is based around regional franchises. Franchises can select products to stock and at what price, which lets them match regional tastes and affluence. Changing this model would be costly for WFF and could lead to increased prices for customers.

After you've reduced the list of issues, the final step is to prioritize them and present them to the development team.

Prioritizing and reporting

How you communicate the results of user testing to the rest of your team is key. It's easy to overwhelm and demoralize them or set them off on an ill-considered campaign of fixes.

If you want people to actually read the results of your usability study, the report needs to be short. A page or two is usually adequate to communicate the issues that need addressing. You can always provide additional supporting evidence if people need convincing. The primary aim of the report is to list the issues and propose possible solutions.

You must also consider the layout of your report. It can't consist of just a list of issues. You need to provide some level of prioritization. This prioritization is based on two factors: the complexity of the fix and the seriousness of the problem. I suggest having two sections entitled "Quick wins" and "Deal breakers."

Quick wins are minor issues that are so easy to fix, it's silly not to. A good example is a poorly named link that makes a user pause for thought. It didn't stop the user from completing the task and so can't be considered crucial. Yet it's so simple to rename the link that there is no reason not to.

Deal breakers prevent users from proceeding further. A classic example is a user who can't find the checkout button on an e-commerce site. Without it, they're unable to continue and are forced to give up. These are priority issues that *must* be fixed.

Not all issues fall neatly into these two categories. Much of the time, users who encounter problems manage to muddle through, which isn't necessarily bad. From childhood, we have all learned that muddling through and experimenting is a great way to learn. When you first watch a test session, you may be horrified by the peculiar way some users interact with your website. It isn't necessary to address every occurrence where a user deviates from your

Quick wins

Some usability fixes are so simple that there is no reason not to do them. For example, removing an unnecessary Cancel button can prevent users from accidentally clicking the wrong button and losing the data they have added.

How can we help?

cancel   send inquiry

expectations. As long as they complete the task and do so without becoming frustrated, you don't need to worry.

These issues aren't deal breakers, because users succeed in overcoming them. But they aren't necessarily quick wins either. Depending on the fix, they may be difficult to overcome.

In effect, these are a third category of *additional issues* that can be addressed after the quick wins and deal breakers. Depending on the size and complexity of the web project, it may be necessary to prioritize these still further, but in most cases they can be grouped together.

With your three categories defined, you have the structure for your report. All that is left is to populate these categories with the issues and proposed solutions. This report can then be discussed with your team.

Where possible, sit down with your team face to face and talk through your findings. This not only ensures that everybody has read the report but enables you to provide some context for the issues described. Finally, this meeting provides an opportunity to plan together how to overcome the problems.

Ecommerce sample usability report

Quick Wins

Disorientated users

Problem: Users had trouble identifying which pages they had already visited. Several users became frustrated when they continually visited the same page.

Proposed solution: Consistently name pages in link text, thereby clearly identifying the destination page. Also visually distinguish between visited and unvisited links.

Concerns about return policy

Problem: Several users seemed concerned about whether goods could be returned but found no information on the site dealing with this issue.

Proposed solution: Write a FAQ on the return policy, and create a prominent link to this page from all key locations (homepage, shopping basket, and checkout).

Deal Breakers

Failure to register address information

Problem: At checkout, several people failed to register their address information because they included a space in their postcode. This was not recognized by the system. After repeated error messages, they gave up.

Proposed solution: Ideally update the technology to accept spaces in postcodes. At the very least show an example postcode and instructions on how to enter them correctly.

Additional Issues

Hard to find contact information

Problem: Users failed to find the contact page in 3 out of 5 cases. Those who did find the page took several attempts.

Proposed solution: Make the contact page a top-level section, and include basic contact information on every page on the site.

A usability report should be short and easy to digest. Organize it into quick wins, deal breakers, and additional issues. Explain each issue succinctly, and suggest a solution.

Next actions

Usability testing can be hugely beneficial without putting a strain on your budget or schedule. You should have a clear understanding of how to run a test session and the role of facilitator. You need to know who to recruit and when to test in the process. Finally, you must be equipped to analyze the results and report back to the rest of the team.

With all that knowledge at your disposal, it's time to create a usability test schedule. This involves three actions:

ACTION 1: *Identify test points during development.* We've already discussed the need to test throughout the development process. Now is the time to add test points to your project plan. Are you going to test the initial design concepts? Will you produce a wireframe and test that? What about initial prototypes? Is there time in the plan for pre-launch testing? Scheduling testing up front decreases the likelihood of it getting squeezed out.

ACTION 2: *Plan your post-launch testing.* Testing shouldn't stop when the site goes live. Organizations continually assess the usability and effectiveness of their sites. This is particularly true when a site has ongoing development. Plan regular review sessions every few months to ensure that quick tweaks made to the site don't create stumbling blocks for users.

ACTION 3: *Create a culture of ad hoc testing.* Although scheduled testing is great, also foster a culture of ongoing ad hoc testing. Constantly ask friends and colleagues to take a quick look at your site. When speaking to your customers, get their feedback; and maybe schedule time for a test session after customer meetings. Wherever possible, get people outside of the development team to look at your site.

A user-centric approach has become best practice within web design over the last few years. But best practice also exists in the way your site is built, as the next chapter will discuss.

7

Ensuring access for all

In this chapter

Being a geek, I love *Star Trek*. I'm sorry, I can't help it. I enjoy the amount of thought that goes into it. Take the difference between the original *Star Trek* series and *Star Trek: The Next Generation*. The original series was like the Wild West. Kirk was a futuristic gunslinger exploring the galaxy, pushing back frontiers, and breaking all the rules. In *Next Generation*, the federation had grown up, and those pioneering days were over. It was about politics and alliances. New discoveries were happening, but at a slower pace.

I bring up *Star Trek* in order to make a comparison. The early days of the web were like the original series: there were no rules, everything was new, and we were flying by the seat of our pants. Now, the web has matured. Like *Next Generation*, you have your own prime directives. These include accessibility, standards, and legal requirements. Web design has grown up a lot. Unfortunately, a lot of Kirks remain, building websites like it's 1999.

This chapter will help you make sure your website is accessible to everyone from search engines and disabled users to those wishing to print your web pages or access them from a mobile devices. It will explain best practice and ensure that you don't get caught by cowboy designers peddling out-of-date techniques.

IDENTIFY THE COWBOYS

In order to identify cowboy designers and create an accessible site, you need to understand best practice. Before I can help you do that, I need to begin with a history lesson.

Learning from history

When Tim Berners-Lee proposed the World Wide Web back in the early 1990s, he couldn't have imagined what we have today. Early web pages were purely textual. There were no images and certainly no video. We also had no substantial control over layout or colors. A web page was expected to describe the *meaning* of content, not to dictate its appearance. The appearance of the document was controlled by the browser.

What's New, June 1993

June 27, 1993
Digital Equipment Corporation is running a Web server from their anonymous FTP server. Included are pointers to DEC product information, Ultrix and OSF/1 FAQ's, DEC research reports, and more.

The Army Research Laboratory is now running a Web server. Included is information on the ARL Scientific Visualization effort, a picture of the arrival of a KSR-1 supercomputer at ARL, and more.

Information on the Front Range Consortium is now online -- here's their Web server. Members of the Front Range Consortium include CAPP, NCAR/SCD, and NOAA/FSL.

The Navy Research Laboratory Advanced Concepts Group is now online.

June 25, 1993
A Web server has been installed at the Centre Universitaire d'Informatique of the University of Geneva. Information about various research groups at the CUI is available, as well as a number of other experimental services.

June 24, 1993
The Institute for Theoretical Physics at State University of New York at Stony Brook is now running a Web server. Included are online Institute news bulletins, a directory of people, and local system documentation.

HyTelnet 6.5 is now online; see here.

If you haven't tried it yet, take a look at the Web server running inside JaysHouseMOO. See particularly the object browser. (For those unfamiliar with the term, a MOO is a "consensual text-based virtual reality", aka MUD or Multi-User Dungeon, wherein people interact with one other in a computer-enabled world. Since these systems commonly feature rich and extensible programming environments, it is possible to build Web, Gopher, and other servers (and clients!) directly into the online virtual world. Another example of this is the Gopher server running inside the Actuator MUD; more examples are here.)

June 23, 1993
A new server at Georgia Tech is here; see in particular resources by subject. Most of the stuff in there is off limits to off-site people -- bummer. But not a hypermedia version of The Whistle and information on their Graphics, Visualization, and Useability Lab.

June 22, 1993
A new and greatly improved HTML primer is now online, courtesy of the Publications group at NCSA. Comments to pubs@ncsa.uiuc.edu.

Carnegie Mellon has announced their Web server; here's the "Front Door"; here's the home page. ("Front door"... interesting metaphor, that.) Interesting things on their server include a hypermedia version of CMU technical reports archive, an index of online reference works, an index of online journals, some personal home pages, and more. Also, they're keeping us Mosaic developers in line with their own internal list of Mosaic bugs. (Bugs? Us?)

Early markup provided no control over design. It existed to describe content, not appearance. The browser decided how to display the page.

For example, a heading was marked up with a heading tag like so:

```
<h1>Identifying the cowboys</hi>
```

And a paragraph was marked up using a P tag:

```
<p>While a paragraph would be marked up using a P tag...</p>
```

The browser interpreted this markup by displaying headings in a larger font and putting carriage returns between paragraphs. In short, the web page described the content's *semantic* meaning.

As the web grew in popularity, it became more than a repository of information. It began to be perceived as a marketing tool, and website owners wanted control over the appearance of their pages. Browser manufacturers obliged by introducing support for adding images, controlling colors, and setting fonts. The markup now described the appearance of the page as well as the content. Design and content began to mix.

Even this wasn't enough to satisfy the marketers. They wanted to replicate print designs on the web. This led to the abuse of markup. Instead of tags being used to

In 1997, David Siegel's book *Creating Killer Web Sites* (New Rider) popularized the use of tables for controlling web-page layout. At the time, this appeared to be positive; but in hindsight, it proved detrimental.

describe the meaning of content, they were selected because the browsers displayed them in a particular way. For example, web designers chose an H1 tag not because they wanted to mark up a heading but because they wanted to make text large and bold.

The biggest abuse was in the use of the table tag. The table tag was originally created to display tabular data, similar to most spreadsheets. Web designers quickly discovered that tables could be used to position content on a page with almost to-the-pixel control.

Admittedly, this approach worked. Website owners got the print-like designs they wanted. Software automated the process of creating this spaghetti code and kept development costs low. Where, then, was the problem?

Understanding the consequences of poor code

Unfortunately, design control came at a cost. The complicated, messy markup created by table-based design had ramifications. Web pages became

> Browser specific

> Bloated

> Hard to maintain

Coding for multiple browsers

With browsers displaying this "bastardized code" in slightly different ways and offering support for their own proprietary tags, it became increasingly hard to build sites that were accessible by all. Designers were often forced to present different versions of a site to each browser, thus increasing development time. Designers working with limited budgets sometimes

Yahoo! Music effectively excludes users who aren't using the latest browser.

gave up and supported only a single browser. If the user happened to be using a competing browser or an old version, they were effectively excluded from the site. These badly coded websites sometimes excluded users accessing the internet via an alternative device such as a screen reader (used by people with visual impairments). Table-based code could also exclude those with a slower connection.

Bloated code

Because HTML markup was never intended to produce complex designs, large amounts of additional code were required. The average web page swelled in size and took a considerable time to download.

When broadband arrived, web designers believed that download speed was no longer an issue. But the rise of broadband was accompanied by an increase in web access via mobile devices. These devices typically only have dial-up connection speeds.

Download size is also still an issue for larger, more heavily trafficked websites. A cost is associated with data served from a website. When downloads exceed a certain limit, the hosting provider may start to charge. Tiny amounts of data can make a real difference when they're downloaded many thousand times.

The cost of poor code isn't just financial. There is also a cost in work hours.

Hard-to-maintain code

Complex code was hard to maintain. Even the simplest change, such as altering the size of text, had to be made many hundreds of times across every page on a website.

Website owners once paid web designers ridiculous fees to make changes to content when they should have been able to do it themselves. Many sites have unnecessary content-management systems (CMSs) because the code was too complicated to understand. Sites became obsolete as new browsers were released and broke existing code. It was often more cost effective to throw out a site and start again than to fix what was there.

Fixes were required as browsers updated. Unfortunately because of the complexity of the code these fixes were expensive.

A culture of redesign

The difficulties in maintaining these websites led to a culture of redesign. Every few years, an organization became frustrated with its website and got a web design company to fix the site. Unfortunately, this new site was often just as badly built and also degraded over time as new browsers were released and content wasn't kept up to date. The process then repeated itself.

So far, I've spoken about these problems in the past tense, implying that websites are no longer built this way. But many still are. For a variety of reasons, web designers choose not to keep up with best practice. It falls to you as the client to set the standard of work you require. To do this, you need to understand standards-based design.

Learning a better way to build websites

While web designers were bastardizing markup to suit their needs, Tim Berners-Lee and a group of industry experts (the World Wide Web Consortium [W3C]) were working on a solution to the problem. They proposed a complete separation of content from design. The markup would return to its original role of defining the meaning of content. Meanwhile, a separate file would describe to the browser how that content should look. This file was called a cascading

Designing with Web Standards by Jeffrey Zeldman (Peachpit, 2006) is the definitive introduction to standards-based design. It's ideal for explaining the benefits of standards to designers and developers.

stylesheet (CSS). This separation of content from design provided the design control that website owners demanded, while avoiding the pitfalls of other techniques.

At first, browser support was limited. But thanks to the campaigning of groups like the Web Standards Project, that situation quickly changed. A new generation of web designers emerged, dedicated to building websites that conform to these new best practices. These websites are more likely to be accessible, faster to download, and easier to maintain. They provide a host of additional benefits that are explored in the next section.

Unfortunately, not all web designers are so progressive. Many still produce websites that mix content and design and ignore accessibility. With many clients still ignorant of best practice, these developers have little motivation to change their ways. These clients only care that their site looks OK on their computer—but you should consider the broader picture. Toward that end, I'll endeavor to clearly explain the benefits of standards-based design. Let's begin with control over styling.

A MATTER OF STYLE

The greatest benefit of this new approach to building websites is born out of the separation of design from content. With all design being defined from a single file (the CSS), it's simple to change that file and give your site a different look. The content remains the same, but the site's design can change radically. This offers a host of possibilities, not least when you're printing.

Improving printing

If you've ever printed a web page, you know that printing on the web is less than satisfactory. You have to deal with two fundamental flaws:

> *It wastes paper and ink by printing screen elements that the user doesn't need.* Why print the navigation or interface graphics? These are needed while you're interacting with a website, not for reading a piece of paper.

> *Many websites fail to print properly.* This can manifest in many ways, but the most common is content being truncated down the right side of the page.

Standards-based design resolves these problems by allowing you to specify a different look and feel when printing. By swapping the stylesheet, you can change to a design that prints perfectly and removes the unwanted screen elements. For example, take my

This is how the Boagworld website (http://www.boagworld.com) looks when viewed through a web browser.

This is how the same site looks when printed.

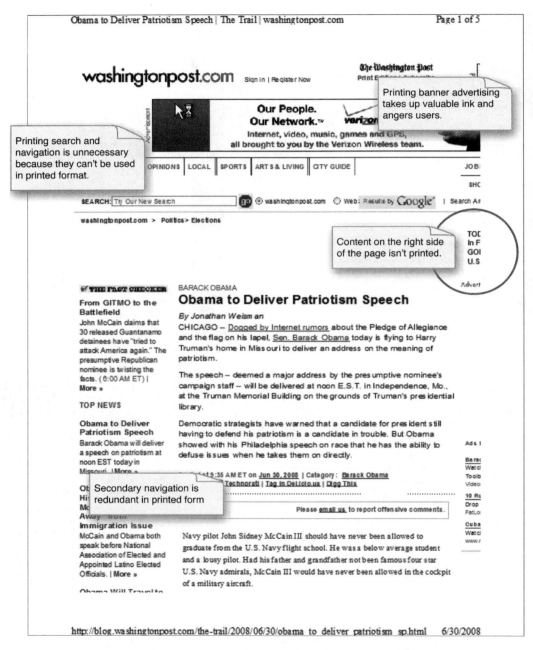

Many websites print poorly. They cut off content and waste both paper and ink. Although users can correct these problems with plug-ins and settings, you should always ensure that your site prints correctly.

own site at boagworld.com. When people print one of my blog posts, all the secondary content and navigation are removed. The site prints only the information users want.

Separation of content from design also helps when you're catering to the emerging mobile sector.

Capturing the emerging market

Cameron Moll, in his e-book *Mobile Web Design*, states that by 2010 it's anticipated that there will be 4 billion mobile-phone subscribers worldwide. That is an astounding 59% of the entire planet's population. The cell phone has existed only 35 years, and yet the cell-phone industry has sold 2.7 billion units. Compared with 850 million personal computers sold over 30 years, this is amazing growth. In the U.S. and U.K., access to the web from a mobile device accounts for between 17% and 19% of web usage. These figures are set to increase.

In chapter 12, "Planning for the future," we'll look at harnessing this emerging market. For now, all you need to know is that separating content from design is a key part of the process. Separation lets you deliver a mobile-friendly stylesheet to mobile devices without the need to maintain multiple sites.

The ability to swap styles is only the tip of the iceberg. Separating content from design also allows your website to adapt based on circumstances.

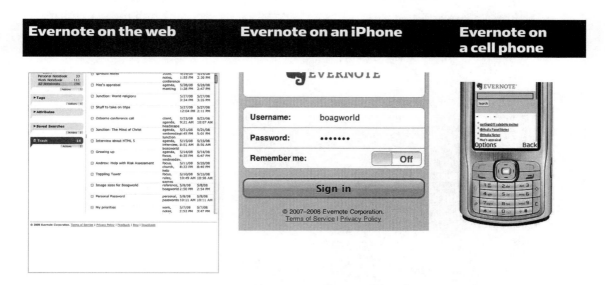

Evernote.com uses standards to help bring different visual experiences to a variety of devices.

Responding quickly to change

Traditionally, websites have been difficult to change. When content and design are mixed, a small change like altering the default font size requires every page on the site to be edited. When you use standards, this is no longer the case—and that offers a wealth of advantages.

Imagine you're launching a new advertising campaign that has a different look and feel from the rest of your brand. Using standards-based design, you can change the entire site to match this design and swap back when the campaign is over.

You can also style the site depending on where the user is referred from. If they come from a partner's website, your site can be rebranded to match their style. This provides a seamless experience for the user.

The real power of standards isn't in complete redesigns but in the ongoing evolution of your site. Standards make it easy to continually improve your site based on user feedback. If people complain that links are hard to read, then you can quickly change them. If users can't find the search bar, you can restyle it. The ability to make quick, incremental changes in response to user requirements provides a competitive edge.

Standards also provide tangible improvements to the accessibility of your site.

Jason Santa Maria uses stylesheet switching to customize the design of his site to suit the content of each page.

NEVER TURN AWAY USERS (OR GOOGLE)

A common response I hear when talking about web accessibility is that it "doesn't apply to us because we don't have any blind users." Setting aside the obvious absurdity of this statement (you won't have blind users if your site is inaccessible), it demonstrates a fundamental misunderstanding of what web accessibility is about.

Web accessibility shouldn't stop at access for the blind. In fact, you shouldn't focus solely on access for the disabled. Everyone should have access to the web whether they use a screen reader because of a visual impairment or a mobile device with poor connection speeds and text-only support. Access should be available regardless of device, connection, or disability.

When you have this mindset, the importance of separating content from design becomes more obvious. Although your content remains the same, its presentation needs to change based on user requirements. A mobile device with a small screen requires a different design solution than a desktop computer. A screen reader requires no design at all, whereas someone with low vision may want larger text. All of this is straightforward when design and content are separate.

Recognizing that accessibility is about access for all brings even greater realizations—particularly from a financial perspective.

Handling the expense of accessibility

A big objection to providing an accessible site is the expense. Quotes to make a site "accessible" often seem disproportionately high when compared to the financial returns from a minority disabled audience.

In reality, this reasoning is flawed. First, the high cost of "making a site accessible" is normally associated only with sites built using out-of-date techniques. When a site separates content and design, it's inherently more accessible. Also, the cost of further improving that accessibility is significantly less. Second, as we've already established, accessibility isn't just about the disabled; return on investment will be significantly higher than if you focus only on disabled users.

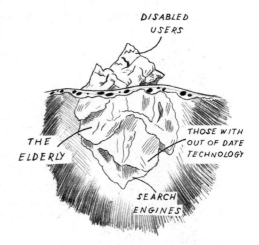

Disability is the tip of the access iceberg. Accessibility also including meeting the needs of the elderly, those with out-of-date technology, and the unique requirements search engines have when indexing your site.

In the United Kingdom alone, it's estimated that those registered as disabled have a spending power of more than $160bn. Add to this those not registered as disabled but with physical or cognitive conditions that affect their use of the web. The elderly are a great example of this audience: as you age, your vision declines, as do your motor skills, making websites increasingly difficult to use.

Even if you stop there, this constitutes a significant audience that you're potentially turning away from your website. When you add those using dial-up connections, working on older computers, or lacking the latest plug-in, it quickly becomes apparent that access for all can't be ignored.

Imagine turning away customers from a restaurant because they're too old or suffer from color blindness. You wouldn't do it. Why then do you turn people away on the web?

You aren't just turning away users. If your site isn't built using best practices, you may also be turning away search engines.

A restaurant owner would never turn away paying customers, so why should your website?

Achieving increased traffic with minimum effort

In many ways, a search engine like Google is the ultimate disabled user. It can't see, and has only limited support for more advanced web features such as video and audio. It's easy to build a site that is either totally or partially inaccessible to Google.

Search engines are interested in only one thing: providing relevant results to their users. They only look at the content. They don't care about design or advanced web features.

If you want your website to rank highly on search engines, you need to ensure that they can access your content. Building with best practices and accessibility in mind will do that.

By separating design from content, you make it easier for a search engine to catalogue your site. If you mark up that content semantically (describing the headings, and so on), you make it easier for search engines to understand what the page is about.

Finally, many of the techniques used to improve disabled access also help search engines. For example, blind users can't see images, so a hidden description is associated with each picture. This is called an **ALT** attribute. It tells the user what is contained within the image—and it tells search engines the same thing.

```
<img src="pic.jpg" alt="Paul and
James in front of Arthur's Seat,
Edinburgh" />
```

The ALT attribute describes the content of an image. This is important for visually impaired users but also helps with search-engine indexing.

Many organizations pay large sums of money to improve their ranking on search engines while ignoring accessibility as "not cost effective." If they spent the money on best practices, they could have both. In chapter 10, "Driving traffic," we'll explore more ways to promote your site. For now, you need to be aware that accessibility can help with your search-engine rankings.

Accessibility can provide financial benefits by increasing the amount of traffic going to your site and allowing more of those visitors to gain access. But that isn't the only reason to worry about accessibility. There are also potential legal obligations.

EXCEED YOUR LEGAL OBLIGATIONS

Fear of litigation is the most common motivating factor for addressing a website's accessibility. From lobby groups campaigning for disabled rights to web designers trying to drum up business, there is no shortage of people saying your site is breaking the law. Most of these claims are extreme; and although some could potentially be true, they do little to encourage best practice.

I'm not a lawyer and have no intention of giving legal advice about your liability. The varying legislation on web accessibility worldwide makes that impossible. What I can share with you is my experience and what I have observed online.

You probably have a legal obligation to provide an accessible website. Whether it's Section 508 in the U.S. or the Disability Discrimination Act in the U.K., most countries have some form of legislation to address the issue of online accessibility. But even if your website contravenes the legislation, you won't necessarily be taken to court.

A more likely scenario is that you'll receive a complaint about some aspect of your site. How you respond to that complaint will dictate whether you end up in court. Failure to respond quickly or take the complaint seriously could lead to litigation. If you respond quickly and apologetically, then chances are the user will go away happy.

Am I proposing that you ignore web accessibility until somebody complains? Certainly not. I hope I've already demonstrated good reasons to address accessibility beyond legal requirements. I merely wish to dispel the fear-mongering that surrounds this subject.

This kind of fear-mongering demands all or nothing. You must comply with legislation today or face the consequences. This can seem overwhelming, and many people give up without trying. They choose instead to take the risk that nobody will draw attention to the failings of their site.

How you handle complaints will dictate whether your organization ends up in court.

Instead, I believe website owners should start small and improve accessibility over time. A large proportion of accessibility problems can be overcome with a few simple fixes.

There is no lack of people suggesting ways to ensure your site's accessibility, from government legislation to pressure groups and disability charities. The best solution lies with the World Wide Web Consortium (W3C). In addition to producing the specifications for HTML, CSS, and other aspects of standards-based design, the W3C has also produced extensive guidelines on accessibility. That is why accessibility and standards are so closely linked.

The guidelines produced by the W3C have become the template for almost all other accessibility advice. The first guidelines published by the W3C came out in 1999 and were referred to as WCAG 1. Since then, the web has moved on considerably, so the W3C has produced a second version called WCAG 2.

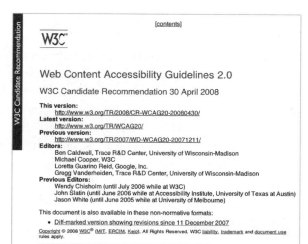

The Web Content Accessibility Guidelines 2.0 (WCAG 2) are the definitive template for web accessibility going forward.

At first glance, the W3C guidelines can be intimidating. The documentation associated with them is extensive and highly technical in places. But the guidelines themselves are relatively easy to understand. They're broken down into four principles regarding content:

> *Perceivable*—Elements on your website must be presentable to users in ways they can perceive.

> *Operable*—User must be able to navigate and use your website.

> *Understandable*—Your website must be easy to understand.

> *Robust*—Content must be robust enough that it can be accessed by a variety of different devices.

These are all common sense. Then, each of the four areas is segmented into specific ways you can achieve it. For example, under "Perceivable" is a guideline that reads "Provide text alternatives for any non-text content so that it can be changed into other forms people need, such as large print, Braille, speech, symbols or simpler language."

W3C guidelines appear intimidating, but the core principles are easy to grasp.

Each guideline is written in language that is relatively easy to understand, and I recommend you take the time to read them all. The guidelines are divided into individual success criteria, but this technical detail isn't relevant to you as a website owner.

Understanding the guidelines is important for two reasons. First, it makes it easier to ensure that any web designer you hire knows the latest accessibility techniques. Shortcomings are obvious when you're aware of what is required. Second, you need to understand the basics of accessibility if you wish to create an accessibility policy for your organization.

CREATE AN ACCESSIBILITY POLICY

As I've said, many organizations embrace accessibility not due to a desire to improve access, but from a fear of litigation. This leads to a "butt-covering" mentality. They fixate on a set of guidelines (like WCAG) and blindly check every box until they have fully conformed with the specification.

This approach is flawed because it's organizationally focused rather than user focused. Following generic guidelines that may or may not apply to your users' specific needs is wasteful and serves nobody.

A better approach is to use WCAG as a starting point for the creation of an accessibility policy. This outlines your organization's approach to dealing with issues of accessibility and should include the following:

> Your ultimate objectives in terms of W3C guidelines

> A roadmap for reaching these objectives

> A process for testing compliance with these objectives

> A plan for maintaining the accessibility of your site over time

> A procedure for responding to complaints

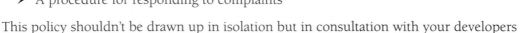

Many organizations only choose to comply with the W3C accessibility guidelines in order to avoid prosecution.

This policy shouldn't be drawn up in isolation but in consultation with your developers (who must implement the objectives) and your content providers (whose help will be vital if your site is to remain accessible). Let's look at each of the elements that appear in your accessibility policy.

Establishing your long-term accessibility goal

Every accessibility policy should have an end goal in mind. This objective will probably change over time, but there is value in documenting your current aim. What that aim should be comes from discussion with developers, content providers, and end users. But it will probably be based on some aspect of WCAG 2.

Each WCAG 2 guideline is broken down into one or more success criteria. These criteria are rated according to their level of conformance. There are three levels: A, AA, and AAA.

The three levels of web accessibility

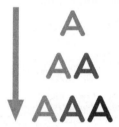

Level A (also known as Priority 1) - A website **must** satisfy this checkpoint. Otherwise, one or more groups will find it *impossible* to access information.

Level double-A (also known as Priority 2) - A website **should** satisfy this checkpoint. Otherwise, one or more groups will find it *difficult* to access information.

Level triple-A (also known as Priority 3) - A website **may** address this checkpoint. Otherwise, one or more groups will find it *somewhat difficult* to access information.

Traditionally, organizations have decided to reach a certainly level across all guidelines. For example, a company may aim to make an entire site Level AA compliant. Depending on your circumstances, this may prove difficult to achieve. A better approach is to aim for a minimum of Level A across the board but seek to comply to higher levels of accessibility on some guidelines. This more tailored approach take into account the varying requirements of your business, content, and audience.

Of course, identifying an end goal is one thing. Getting there is another.

Having a roadmap for overcoming common problems

Even achieving the most basic level of accessibility (Level A) can be challenging if you're implement it on an existing website. It is far cheaper and easier to plan with accessibility in mind from the outset. But when you don't have that luxury, you don't need to immediately implement Level A. Your accessibility policy can outline a roadmap for achieving longer-term goals.

The *Pareto principle* or *80/20 rule* (http://en.wikipedia.org/wiki/Pareto_principle) states that for many events, 80% of the effects come from 20% of the causes. This holds true for accessibility, where a small number of issues cause the vast majority of problems. It's logical to start any roadmap by resolving these issues first—but what are they? That is a subjective question, but here are the most common problems I encounter:

Poorly described images

I've mentioned that images should have associated **ALT** attributes. This benefits both visually impaired users and search-engine placement. But the problem of poorly described images isn't due only to a lack of description. It's also caused by badly written descriptions.

Because many people realize the benefit of **ALT** attributes for search-engine placement, they fill these descriptions with keywords and make them overly long. You should make sure all content images have an **ALT** attribute and that it clearly describes what is being shown in a single sentence. Longer descriptions can be annoying when read back by a screen reader.

But it isn't just images that are labeled badly; so are links.

Badly labeled links

The text in a link should describe that link without context. Screen readers can read all the links on a page as a single list, which helps users quickly navigate without listening to the entire page. The problem arises when a link is entitled "click here," which doesn't give the user any information about where the link leads. A better link would read "latest news." Where a longer description is required, a `title` attribute (similar to an **ALT** attribute) can provide more information.

Using descriptive links helps not only screen-reader users but also users who are quickly scanning a page looking for the next link to follow. And search engines use the content of a link as a way of judging what the page linked to is about.

If a link is labeled "click here," it's meaningless out of context. For visually impaired users, this can be frustrating.

In addition to describing links and images, you also need to consider other forms of media.

No alternatives to media

When you're using video, audio, or any form of media that requires additional plug-ins, you need to provide an alternative version. This alternative should be in the form of either a transcript (in the case of audio) or captions (in the case of video or other media where visuals and audio are synced).

At first glance, this seems like a massive undertaking. But a number of services like Casting Words provide transcription at a reasonable rate, and tools like Overstream (http://www.overstream.net/) can help you create captions.

It's important to provide these alternatives because users may not be able to perceive the content due to technological limitations or disability. This is also true for JavaScript.

Reliance on JavaScript

JavaScript is a programming language that is used to achieve many of the interactions you see on websites. From pop-up windows to services like Google Maps, JavaScript is amazingly flexible and heavily used.

JavaScript itself isn't inaccessible. It exists to add interaction and behavior to a website in the same way HTML provides content and CSS provides design. The problem is in the implementation.

Casting Words (http://Castingwords.com) converts audio to text. This is just one of the services that can help your site become more accessible.

Not everyone has access to JavaScript, and search engines regularly ignore it. It's therefore important that all content is accessible even when JavaScript isn't available. The most common problem is using JavaScript to create navigation and other links. If JavaScript isn't available, it's impossible for users to follow those links to the content beneath. Similarly, when JavaScript is used to add content to a page, this content becomes inaccessible if JavaScript is disabled. Never rely solely on JavaScript as a method of accessing content.

The final accessibility mistake I see regularly is preventing users from resizing text.

Hard-to-read text

By default, all major browsers let users control text size. This is required for users with less than perfect vision. Most visual impairments require font sizes to be increased. But some people need smaller text to fit better within a limited field of view.

Also, many visual impairments are made worse by poor color contrast between the text and background colors.

Although browsers provide the ability to resize text, and it's relatively trivial to design with sufficient contrast, many web designers fail to build with this in mind. When the user resizes text, the design breaks and becomes unreadable. Poor color combinations increase the problem.

The BestBuy site (http://www.bestbuy.com/) doesn't adapt well when users enlarge the text. Screen elements are forced out of position, and text overlaps.

There is no good reason for this beyond laziness. Ensure that your designers consider these issues when developing your site.

By addressing these five problems, you can dramatically improve the accessibility of your website. None of these issues is particularly hard to overcome, and the financial investment is minimal. You'll increase the traffic to your site and the number of visitors able to successfully navigate it.

But an accessibility policy shouldn't just address quick fixes. It should also provide a comprehensive approach to improving and maintaining site accessibility. To do this, it needs to include a degree of accessibility testing.

Testing accessibility

How you intend to test the accessibility of your site should be a fundamental component of any accessibility policy.

Most organizations rely too heavily on automated services. These online services claim to test web accessibility but can only carry out a basic review. For example, they can't ascertain whether descriptions in **ALT** attributes on images are meaningful or merely stuffed with keywords to improve search-engine placement. They're unable to test some guidelines at all—and this is particularly true with WCAG 2.

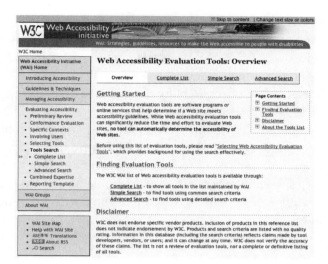

Although they're sometimes misused, accessibility checkers have a role to play. For a list of tools, see http://www.w3.org/WAI/ER/tools/.

There is a place for automated testing. It's useful for identifying potential problems across a large site, but you should never use it in isolation.

User testing with disabled users is far more effective than any amount of automated testing. Granted, finding appropriate disabled users isn't easy, especially when you're faced with a wide range of potential disabilities. Fortunately, a number of organizations can help you with recruitment. They can arrange testing for you and even advise you on how to solve any problems that arise.

Paying for real users may be beyond your budget. If this is the case, ensure that somebody is made responsible for regularly testing the accessibility of your site through a mixture of manual quality control and automated testing.

Whatever approach you adopt, make sure it's documented in your accessibility policy, including how often you intend to test. Frequent testing is important because although it's easy to launch an accessible website, such a site can be difficult to maintain.

Maintaining accessibility

Maintaining the accessibility of your site can be problematic if it's being updated on a regular basis. It's even more complex if multiple people are involved in adding content. Your accessibility policy should address how to maintain accessibility over the long term. You can do so in three ways:

> Regular testing (as explained earlier)

> Training

> Using the right technology

The most important of these is training. Ensure that your development team and content providers understand the basic rules of accessibility. Content providers may only need a set of simple rules to follow. Your development team, on the other hand, will need a deeper understanding and may require formal training.

Unfortunately, a good understanding of accessibility doesn't help when technology fails to produce accessible code. This is especially important when you use a CMS. Make sure your CMS can output clean, accessible code and that wherever possible it enforces accessibility on content editors (such as requiring **ALT** attributes to be defined for images). This is certainly an important point to consider when procuring a CMS.

No matter how good your testing and maintenance plan, problems will arise, and you may receive complaints. How you respond to those complaints will determine whether you find yourself in court.

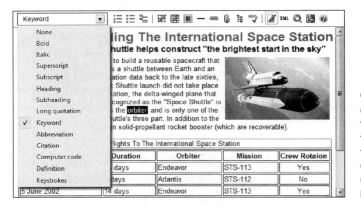

One accessibility weaknesses of many CMSs is the editor. Although the CMS produces accessible code, the editor allows content providers to undo this good work. Consider using an editor like XStandard (http://xstandard.com), which was built with accessibility in mind.

Dealing with complaints

Your accessibility policy should establish the following:

> *Who is responsible for dealing with complaints*—If this isn't clearly defined, complaints often remain unanswered. If a user doesn't receive a response because nobody saw it as "their job," they're more likely to turn to litigation.

> *How quickly your organization should respond to initial complaints*—The person responsible for responding to complaints often has other responsibilities. An email from an angry user may not come high on their list of priorities. To ensure a quick response, set targets in the accessibility policy. This will prevent emails from being forgotten.

> *The process for addressing a complaint*—What happens when a complaint is received? Who estimates the amount of work required to fix the problem? Who signs off on the expenditure? Who is contacted if legal advice is required? These kinds of questions should be answered in your policy.

> *What to do if the complaint can't be addressed*—Sometimes an accessibility issue can't be fixed, or the cost of doing so would be prohibitive. In such cases, a decision must be made about how to respond. This is where it's necessary to open a dialogue with the person complaining. Ask them how they believe the problem could be resolved. Offer them alternative methods of getting the same information (printed brochure, phone, and so on). If you can explain the problem and offer a compromise, most people will be happy. The important thing is to address the complaint and not just hope it goes away.

Dealing with complaints quickly and efficiently should not only avoid litigation but also create improved customer loyalty. Users who encounter problems that are then resolved quickly view a website in a more positive light then if they hadn't encountered the problem at all.

Next actions

This chapter started by demonstrating the importance of accessibility and standards. It then went on to identify elements you should address in these areas. The emphasis has been on informing, rather than encouraging specific actions, because the implementation of standards and accessibility is done by your development team rather than yourself. That said, I encourage you to complete the following three steps:

ACTION 1: *Get your team on board.* The first and most important step is to ensure that your developers and content providers understand the importance of standards and accessibility. If you're recruiting an outside agency, be sure they're using modern techniques. If you have in-house staff, use the content of this chapter to argue for best practice and then consider training to bring people up to speed. If you don't convince your staff, then development will be an uphill battle.

ACTION 2: *Create an accessibility policy.* Begin by writing a rough draft yourself. Don't worry too much about specifics at this stage, but concentrate on creating a skeleton for discussion. Next, sit down with your development team and review the current state of the site. In particular, look at the common accessibility issues and identify which ones need to be addressed. Also discuss with your developers what they consider an achievable goal for site accessibility. Finally, work with your content providers on a training program that will ensure accessibility over the long term.

ACTION 3: *Finish what you start.* After you've completed these actions, consider your long-term strategy for ensuring accessibility. Draw up a periodic test plan, preferably using real disabled users. Also ensure that somebody is ultimately responsible for the ongoing accessibility of your site. Ideally, this person should come from your development team and thus understand the technical detail.

I recognize that some of what I've suggested in this chapter may be overkill for smaller organizations, but you should be able to tailor the discussion to your needs. The key is ensuring accessibility over the long term—and to a large extent, that depends on the tools you use. This brings us nicely to content management systems.

8

Taking control

In this chapter

In the early days of the web, website owners had no control over their sites. They relied on a web designer to make all changes, no matter how basic. Many web designers took advantage of this reliance, charging exorbitant fees to make even the smallest alteration to copy.

Over time, things changed. You no longer needed to know HTML in order to add a phone number or correct a spelling mistake. Tools existed that helped do the job. But they were primitive, and it was still easy to break your site.

You now have a plethora of tools at your disposal, from blogs to enterprise-level content management systems. The question is no longer "How can I edit my website?" but "Which tool is best for me?"

Although a content management system (CMS) isn't a silver bullet, it offers many benefits. This chapter explores those benefits, identifies the drawbacks, and guides you through selecting the right CMS for your organization.

Let's begin this journey by asking a simple question: Do you need a CMS?

THE PROS AND CONS OF A CMS

You may have preconceived ideas about whether you need a CMS. Maybe you believe your site is too small to justify the expense. Alternatively, you may be overwhelmed by content updates and convinced that a CMS will solve all your woes.

Whatever the case, it's important to examine the pros and cons of a CMS. Making the wrong choice can have long-term ramifications for your site.

Let's begin by looking at what makes CMSs so attractive.

The benefits of a CMS

CMSs have become popular over the last few years. Now, even the most basic CMS provides the following:

A CMS isn't always necessary, especially for smaller websites.

> *A lower barrier to entry*—A CMS lets anyone with basic computer skills edit a website. It's no longer necessary to know HTML or understand specialist applications. If you can use a word processor, you can edit a website.

> *Decentralized management*—A lower barrier of entry means that managing web content can be distributed across the organization rather than resting with a few web specialists. Because most CMSs are browser-based, this editing can be done anywhere at any time.

> *A reduction in management costs*—With maintenance shared across the organization, it become less necessary to employ web experts.

> *Faster updates*—Without the bottleneck of a web team and the time involved in briefing that team, updates happen more quickly. A CMS also makes it considerably easier to implement site-wide changes such as updating navigation or editing the site's footer.

> *Greater control*—A CMS gives you control over permissions, making it possible to restrict who can edit which page. More advanced systems also allow workflow, which means pages can be made live only after they're approved by specific individuals.

> *Consistency of design*—Having multiple users updating a site's content can lead to inconsistencies in presentation. A CMS addresses this through the use of templates that standardize the design.

More sophisticated solutions, like those explored later in the chapter, provide even greater benefits. But this list makes it obvious why overworked web teams are attracted to CMSs. CMSs are even more attractive to organizations that pay external agencies to update their sites.

A CMS can look like the ideal solution when content is out of date and nobody has the time or skills to update it. Why, then, do so many organizations complain about their CMS? Although the benefits of a CMS are obvious, the drawbacks are harder to spot. But they do exist, and they can come as a painful shock if you aren't prepared.

A CMS can look like a lifesaver to a web team sinking under website updates.

The drawbacks of a CMS

Before you decide whether to adopt a CMS, or which CMS to choose, you first need to be aware of the hidden costs. These include the following:

> The cost of training

> The affect on quality

> The affect on functionality

> The cost of redundancy and flexibility

> The cost of commitment

It's important that you understand the impact of each.

The cost of training

No matter how well designed the application or how good the documentation, some level of training is required. Training is particularly important with free open-source systems. These tend to have less documentation, and the interfaces are often designed by programmers rather than user-experience experts. The result is a steep learning curve.

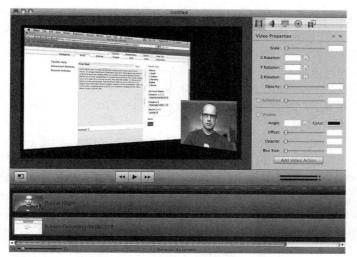

Video tutorials are an effective accompaniment to training. They can be produced inexpensively using tools like ScreenFlow for the Mac or Camtasia Studio for Windows.

The more content production is delegated, the more people you need to train. Whether this is done through onsite training or video tutorials, it's a considerable cost. And organizations often fail to consider that training is an ongoing cost—the more people using a system, the higher the likelihood that someone will need to be replaced.

This ongoing cost isn't limited to training new CMS users. Existing content providers will also require refresher courses if they don't use the CMS regularly. I've often provided training for an organization only to receive a call six months later because people have forgotten how to log in.

Ultimately, the price of having a lot of people editing your site is the cost of increased training. But that isn't the only cost that grows with your numbers.

The affect on quality

What a CMS gives with one hand, it often takes away with the other. Quality and control are classic examples of this problem. Enterprise-level CMSs have complex workflow tools that prevent new content from going live until it has been double-checked for quality.

Before going live, many organizations insist that content be reviewed and approved. Although this maintains quality, it can create a bottleneck.

The problem with this is twofold. First, such functionality is usually found in more expensive systems. Second, few organizations implement this kind of quality control, because doing so creates a bottleneck in the approval process. This bottleneck is precisely the kind of problem a CMS was supposed to *solve*.

This highlights a substantial problem with CMSs: they're often implemented in the hope that they will solve what is an organizational rather than a technical problem. Unfortunately, technology can't solve everything.

At one extreme, you can open up your CMS to let anyone post to your site. Doing so will lead to a decline in the quality of your content. On the other hand, you can limit access and create a bottleneck because only one or two individuals can make content live. The technology offers you lots of options along that sliding scale. You need to find a happy medium.

At least a CMS offers this control, unlike an HTML-driven website. But a non-CMS-driven site gives you more flexibility when it comes to functionality.

The affect on functionality

When your website isn't built on a CMS, the possibilities are endless. Because you have complete control over your code, it's possible to build any additional functionality you require. But when you commit to a CMS, the situation becomes more complex.

Although it's possible to build additional functionality that sits alongside your CMS, you may have problems with integration. For example, if your CMS doesn't have a forum and you wish to add one, you may have to ask users to log in twice. Equally, you may find it hard to tie your CMS in with other systems that you purchase later.

Some CMSs provide plug-ins for additional functionality. But often you're forced to either compromise or wait until the next release of the CMS and hope it supports your requirements.

Users of the Dell website are required to log in twice: once to access their account and once for the forum. This is because the site's underlying technologies don't work together.

Although you may find yourself frustrated by a lack of functionality, it's also possible to be frustrated by too much.

The cost of redundancy and complexity

Unless you have a CMS developed to your exact requirements, it will probably contain functionality you don't need.

It's a problem that Microsoft Word has suffered from for years. Word is powerful and provides an enormous range of features. Yet the majority of people use only a fraction of what is available. Most pay for functionality they don't use and struggle to learn a complex application. This is the problem many CMSs face.

People haven't stopped using Word in favor of a simpler solution because they've invested both money and time in it. This brings us to the final drawback of CMSs.

Like Microsoft Word, many CMSs can appear massively complex because they include functionality that few people use.

The cost of commitment

CMSs demand a high level of commitment on many fronts. These include the following:

> The up-front financial investment in implementing the system

> The cost and time involved in training staff

> The substantial amount of data entered into the system

The third area can be particularly tricky. After your content is in a CMS, getting it out isn't a simple matter.

With such an investment in both time and money, it's important to make the right selection. Changing your mind later is expensive.

Am I suggesting that you avoid CMSs entirely? Not at all. The benefits they provide are real and can't be ignored. Go into the process of selecting a CMS with your eyes wide open: a CMS isn't a magic bullet that solves all your content woes, but it can be a useful tool if selected carefully.

How do you make that selection? You begin by establishing your requirements.

ESTABLISH YOUR REQUIREMENTS

When I left home for college, my mother taught me a valuable lesson. If you want to save money, never go grocery shopping when you're hungry, and always write a list. If you don't, you'll be tempted to buy things you don't need.

The same principle is true when it comes to selecting a CMS. Without a clearly defined set of requirements, you may be seduced by fancy functionality that you'll never use. Before you know it, you'll be buying an enterprise-level system for tens of thousands of dollars when a free blogging tool would have sufficed.

How do you establish your list of requirements? Although your circumstances will vary, 10 areas are particularly important:

> Core functionality

> User interaction

> The editor

> Roles and permissions

> Ability to manage assets

> Versioning

> Search

> Multiple-site support

> Customization

> Multilingual support

Avoid creating a wish list. Think back to chapter 3, "The perfect team," and the advice I gave about writing a brief. Keep your requirements to a minimum, but at the same time keep an eye on the future. You don't want to pay for functionality you never use, but you don't want to be stuck with a CMS that no longer meets your needs and those of your customers.

Let's look at the areas you *should* consider.

Core functionality

When most people think of content management, they think of creating, deleting, editing, and organizing pages. They assume all CMSs do this, and they take this functionality for granted. That isn't necessarily the case. There is also no guarantee that a CMS does any of these things in an intuitive fashion.

Carefully consider your requirements before looking at CMSs. This will ensure that you aren't seduced by unwanted features.

Not all blogging platforms let the owner manage and organize pages into a tree hierarchy. Instead, the individual posts are automatically organized by criteria such as date or category. Although this keeps the interface easy to understand, in some circumstances the lack of organizational functionality can be frustrating.

Carefully consider the basic functionality you need. Even if you don't require the ability to structure and organize pages now, you may in the future. Be wary of any system that doesn't let you complete these core activities.

Thousands of CMSs are on the market, most of which offer this core functionality; but they vary widely in usability. Always test a system for usability before you make a purchase; opensourceCMS.com lets you try a number of options.

The editor is one core feature worth a test drive.

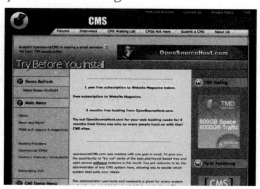

OpensourceCMS (http://opensourcecms.com) is a superb site for demoing CMSs. It has a substantial number of CMS installations that you can try for free.

The editor

The majority of CMSs have a What You See Is What You Get (WYSIWYG) editor. Strangely, this editor is often ill-considered, even though it's the most-used feature within the system.

Traditional WYSIWYG editors give the content provider the ability to customize the appearance of a page to such an extent that it can undermine the consistency of design and branding as discussed in chapter 4 ("Differences over design"). To achieve this level of design control, the CMS mixes design and content. As we established in chapter 7, "Ensuring access for all," this is undesirable.

Wordpress is one of the most popular blogging solutions. It's extremely powerful and completely free of charge. But its default WYSIWYG editor should be replaced with something that encourages more semantic markup, especially when it's being used by less experienced users.

The new generation of editors takes a different approach. The content provider uses the editor to mark up headings, lists, links, and other elements without dictating how they should appear.

Ensure that your list of requirements includes an editor that uses this approach and doesn't give content providers control over appearance. At the least, look for a CMS that lets you replace the editor with a more appropriate solution.

The editor should also be able to handle external assets, such as images and downloads.

Ability to manage assets

Some CMS packages are bad at handling images and files. Issues of accessibility and ease of use can cause frustration with such systems. Ensure that the CMS you select forces the content provider to add **ALT** attributes to images unless they are purely there for decoration. You may also want a CMS that provides basic image-editing tools such as crop, resize, and rotate. But finding such a CMS can be a challenge.

Also consider how the CMS deals with uploading and attaching PDFs, Word documents, and similar files. How are they displayed to users? What descriptions can you attach to the files? Can the search index them?

Search

Approximately half of users begin with search when looking for content. But the search functionality available in CMSs is often inadequate. Here are a few things to look for when assessing search functionality:

> *Freshness*—How often does the search engine index your site? This is especially important if your site changes regularly.

> *Completeness*—Does it index the entire content of each page? What about attached files such as PDFs and Word, Excel, and Powerpoint documents?

> *Speed*—Some search engines can take forever to return results. This is especially common on large sites.

> *Scope*—Can you limit the scope of search to a particular section of the site or refine search results after they're returned?

> *Ranking*—How does the search engine determine the ranking of results? Can this be customized either by the website owner or by the user?

> ➤ *Customization*—Can you control how results are returned and customize the design?

The issue of customization goes far beyond search.

Customization

Now that you have techniques for separating design and content, the presentation of your content shouldn't be dictated by technology. Unfortunately, many content-management providers have failed to adopt best practice, and their systems produce horrendous code. This places unreasonable constraints on design and seriously affects accessibility.

You need a CMS that gives you flexibility in the way content is returned and presented. Can you return news stories in reverse chronological order? Can you display events on a calendar? Is it possible to extract the latest user comments and display them on the homepage? Flexibility makes a CMS stand out.

Some CMSs don't allow customization. They effectively dictate your site's visual appearance.

Speaking of user comments, it's worth mentioning all forms of user interactions.

User interaction

Chapter 11, "Engaging your visitors," will explore the options available for interacting with your users. But you need to give some consideration to the subject now. If you intend to gather user feedback, your CMS must provide that functionality or allow third-party plug-ins to do so. Equally, if you want a community on your site, then you'll require functionality such as chat, forums, comments, and ratings.

As a minimum, you'll require the ability to post forms and collect the responses. How easy does the CMS make this process? Can you customize the fields, or does doing so require technical expertise? What about the results? Can you specify whom they're emailed to? Can they be written to a database or output as an Excel document? Consider the type of functionality you require, and look for a CMS that supports it.

Ask what tools exist for communicating with your customers. Can you send email newsletters? Can recipients be organized into groups who are mailed individually? What about news feeds and RSS?

RSS

RSS feeds let users keep up to date with changes on lots of websites without visiting each site individually. Such feeds are most commonly used for news stories. Each time a new story is published, the site's RSS feed is updated. If users have subscribed to that feed using a piece of software called a *news aggregator*, they're notified of the change.

RSS feeds are growing in popularity and are quickly becoming an indispensable feature of any CMS.

Finally, consider how you want to manage users. Do you need to reset passwords or set permissions? Do you need to be able to export user information into other systems?

But more than user permissions may need managing. You must also consider permissions for those who edit the site.

Roles and permissions

As the number of content providers increases, you'll want more control over who can edit what. Personnel should be able to post job advertisements but not add content to the homepage. This requires a CMS that supports permissions. Permissions let you specify whether users can edit specific pages or entire sections of the site.

As the number of contributors grows, you may require one individual to review the content being posted to ensure accuracy and consistent tone. Alternatively, content may be input by a junior staff member who requires the approval of someone more senior before making that content live.

It's important to maintain control over who can post what on the website.

In both cases, you need a CMS that supports multiple roles. It can be a simple system with editors and an approver, or a complex system that provides customized roles with different permissions.

Finally, enterprise-level CMSs support entire workflows in which a page update has to go through a series of checkpoints before being allowed to go live. These complex scenarios require the ability to roll back pages to a pervious version.

Versioning

Being able to revert to a previous version of a page allows you to quickly recover if something is posted by accident. Some CMSs have complex versioning that lets you roll back to a specific date. In most cases, this is overkill. The most common use of versioning is to return to the last saved state.

Although this sounds like an indispensable feature, it's rarely used except in complex workflow situations. That said, versioning was once a enterprise-level tool that is now available in most CMSs. This is also true of multisite support.

Multiple-site support

With more CMSs allowing you to run multiple websites from the same installation, multisite support is a must-have feature.

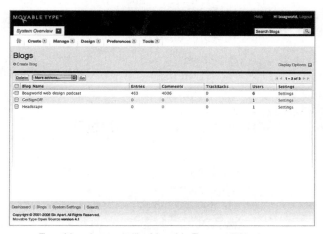

Although you may not currently need to manage more than a single site, that could change. You may decide to launch a new site targeting a different audience. With the growth of the mobile web, you may create a separate site designed for mobile devices. Whatever the reason, having the flexibility to run multiple websites is important.

Even blogging tools like Movable Type and Wordpress support the management of multiple websites.

Another feature that you may not require immediately but could need in the future is multilingual support.

Multilingual support

It's easy to dismiss the need to support multiple languages. Your site may be targeted specifically at the domestic market, or you may sell a language-specific product. Even if your product is language specific, that could change. It's important that your CMS can grow with your business and changing requirements.

Just because you're targeting the domestic market doesn't mean you can ignore language. We live in a multicultural society where numerous languages are spoken. Being able to accommodate these differences provides a significant edge on your competition.

Think through the ramifications of this requirement. Having the ability to add multiple languages doesn't mean you have the content. Too many of my clients have insisted on multilingual support and yet never used it. They failed to consider where they would get the content translated and how they intended to pay for it.

Having a CMS that supports multiple languages doesn't mean you'll be able to deliver a multilingual website.

These suggestions will help you narrow your list of requirements. Now comes the job of examining the different options available.

EXAMINE YOUR OPTIONS

With so many CMSs available, how do you begin to choose? Your list of requirements will help, but you can't compare them against every single system. You need a way to quickly narrow the field.

First, decide if you want to use an existing CMS or get something custom built.

Using an off-the-shelf CMS vs. a custom-built CMS

In most cases, why reinvent the wheel? There is little point in building something from scratch when it's already been built a thousand times before. But there are always exceptions.

A custom build provides your exact requirements and overcomes many of the drawbacks mentioned earlier. A bespoke CMS is completely flexible.

This flexibility can be important when your requirements deviate from the norm. Maybe you have existing systems that your CMS must integrate with. Or perhaps you have an unusual business model that requires your site to work in a specific way. The more your requirements differ from others', the less likely it is that an off-the-shelf system will work for you.

Be careful when using a custom-built CMS.
Ensure that you aren't tied to a single supplier.

Unfortunately, a custom CMS can be expensive. But that isn't the only weakness. Without careful planning, you can find yourself tied to the developer who built the system.

If you're running an off-the-shelf CMS (especially one that's well known), it's relatively easy to change developers if you're unhappy with the service you've received. This isn't the case with bespoke builds.

Without careful documentation, it can be hard for one developer to understand another's code. If you decide to use a bespoke system, ensure that the developer provides adequate documentation so you avoid this problem. Also ask what technology is being used and call around to see if others can support that programming language. If your developer chooses an obscure language, you may have difficulty finding someone who can write in it.

In most cases, you'll work with an off-the-shelf system. If that is your choice, how do you go about narrowing the field?

Choosing a type of CMS

CMSs fall into several broad categories. Although individual systems vary within these categories, each has certain general characteristics. By matching your requirements to one of these broad categories, you help reduce your options considerably. These categories are as follows:

> Desktop applications

> Partial CMSs

> Blogs

> Enterprise-level CMSs

Let's look at the characteristics of each and what features they support.

Desktop applications

Some argue that desktop applications aren't CMSs because they don't manage your content online. But they do manage content and so are worth mentioning.

Products like Adobe Contribute, Dreamweaver, and Microsoft Expression fall into this category. They tend to be relatively cheap, require no special technology on your web server, and are easy to set up.

Desktop applications normally provide an excellent editor, and more modern versions also place their emphasis on marking up the meaning of content rather than defining its appearance. But these applications can fall down on core functionality. Adding and deleting pages can be painful when you're working with large numbers of pages.

Beyond editing, their use is limited. Some offer basic permissions but nothing in terms of versioning, search, or multilingual support.

The use of desktop applications should be restricted to sites that change infrequently.

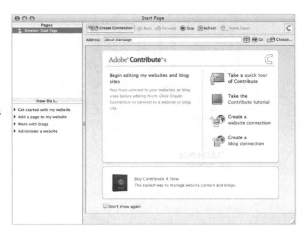

Adobe Contribute is an excellent desktop application for the less-experienced content contributor.

Partial CMSs

Most web pages rarely change. Only specific sections need updating on a regular basis. There is no reason your entire website needs to be built using a CMS. It's possible to combine a desktop application with partial systems to deal with specific functionality. Excellent tools are available for managing news, events, communities, and search.

The downside of this approach is that it can be hard to get these various tools talking to one another. This can become complicated if you use a number of them together.

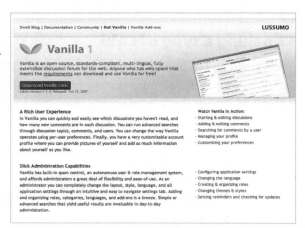

The Vanilla forum (getvanilla.com) is just one of many solutions that provide a portion of the functionality offered by a full CMS.

And despite the number of available tools, they don't cover functionality like versioning, permissions, multisite management, or multilingual support. That said, they're perfect when you have one or two areas of your site that need updating or where you require community features.

Blogging software like Wordpress is installed on your web server. Alternatively, you can use a system like Typepad, which is hosted for you. This is ideal if you don't have a web server capable of hosting software. We'll explore these concepts further in chapter 9, "Decoding technobabble."

Blogs

Blogs are the most common form of CMS. Their core functionality is to publish a series of pages sorted by category and date. This is ideal for managing regularly updated news. Recently, blogs have become considerably more powerful, letting you order pages into hierarchical structures. Many now offer plug-in support for additional functionality.

Blogs normally come with a basic editor that emphasizes appearance over meaning. You may therefore need to replace the editor with something more advanced.

Blogs also lack multilingual support but do let you manage multiple websites. They provide an adequate search function and allow extensive customization.

Blogs are often adequate for smaller organizations. They're especially good at dealing with constantly updating news stories. For larger organizations, a full CMS is more appropriate.

Enterprise-level CMSs

Enterprise-level CMSs are comprehensive solutions that offer the complete suite of functionality from versioning to multilingual support. They often carry a hefty price tag, although open-source solutions are also available.

Most of these CMSs meet my criteria, but the quality of implementation can vary tremendously. You need to look at the options and compare ease of use, power, and flexibility. These full-blown CMSs are ideal for organizations that require a wide range of functionality and have regularly changing content produced by a large numbers of contributors.

After you've established the type of CMS you require, it becomes a matter of comparing and contrasting the options. But you may find a number that are possible candidates. How do you make the final selection?

MAKE YOUR SELECTION

Many CMSs offer similar functionality. After all, most people want similar things. But functionality and price shouldn't be the only criteria by which you make your judgment. You need to consider a number of additional issues:

> Licensing

> The development team

> Security

> Accessibility and code quality

> Documentation and training

> Support

> Community

With so many CMSs offering similar functionality, look at external factors when making your choice.

Licensing

Examine in detail the license attached to your choice of CMS. Some licenses state that you can't change the source code or use an alternative developer.

You may also find that your license is per site or (worse) per user. This can become very expensive if you need to set up multiple sites or have a large number of content contributors. Ideally, you want an agreement that allows unlimited use of the CMS with the exception of reselling.

The development team

Look carefully at the development team behind any CMS you're considering. Is it an open-source project with a community of developers or the product of a single company? Neither approach is wrong, but you need to be confident about the product's long-term health.

Open-source projects can be highly productive despite often being created by volunteers, but they can die off quickly if a more attractive project comes along. If you're considering an open-source solution, look at the age of the product: mature products are more likely to remain supported in the long term.

With a commercial product, you need to be confident about the long-term viability of that company. Consider requesting a copy of its accounts to confirm its financial stability.

In either case, look for a team that regularly releases updates to their system. This is particularly important from a security perspective.

Red Dot is a leading CMS with a committed team of developers. This is apparent from the vibrant community site and frequent patches and updates.

Security

Security is an important issue for any CMS. If your site is hacked, you may lose content or find yourself in litigation if hackers get hold of your users' personal data.

Judging the security of a CMS may require some technical expertise. If you're unsure, get an expert's opinion. At the least, do a Google search on the name of the CMS and "security issues." If you see lots of results, then get an expert opinion.

Accessibility and code quality

As we established in chapter 7, it's important to build using the latest best practice. Doing so ensures that your site is accessible and provides the flexibility to adapt over time.

Judging whether a CMS uses best practice is difficult if you aren't a web designer. Talk to the CMS developers about their approach to accessibility. Equipped with the knowledge from chapter 7, you should be able to get an indication of their competency. But if you have any doubt, look for a CMS that is accredited by a respected third party.

Use what you learned in chapter 7 to speak with CMS suppliers about their approach to accessibility and standards.

One aspect of best practice we have yet to discuss are webpage addresses. For a long time, CMSs produced addresses that looked like this:

http://www.boagworld.com/index.php?sourceid=navclient&q=4

But more recently, content-management developers have realized that such addresses are difficult to read and damage search-engine placement. Modern CMSs produce addresses that look more like this:

http://boagworld.com/technology/friendly_urls/

This is a huge step forward and also lets you use the web address as a navigational tool. Users can identify where they are in the site and edit the URL to find different pages. For example, if the previous address is shortened to http://boagworld.com/technology/, it returns all pages within the technology section.

Whenever possible, look for systems that support friendly URLs. They're a good feature to have and provide an indication of how up-to-date the developers' practices are. If a CMS supports friendly URLs, it may also support accessibility and standards.

Additional information about best practice should be made available through the documentation that supports the CMS. This too is an important differentiating factor.

Documentation and training

Good documentation is a crucial component of any CMS. As I've said, content providers may not use the system on a daily basis. They can easily forget how it works.

Documentation should therefore be comprehensive and easy to use. Some CMSs also provide walkthroughs, video tutorials, and context-sensitive help. These help users better understand how the system operates.

Documentation should also be available for developers. This will enable your web team to adapt the CMS to better suit your needs. Without this documentation, it can be nearly impossible to work out how the CMS can be customized.

Alongside documentation, training is another useful resource. It's important for content providers who need more than a manual before they begin using the system. Training provides hands-on experience and the opportunity to ask questions.

No matter how good the CMS and supporting documentation are, on some occasions you'll require additional support.

Support

You need to ask some hard questions about support. What happens if you identify a bug in the CMS? Will you be required to pay for the fix? How fast can you expect a response? Do you require 24/7 support? You must know your requirements and

understand what the CMS provider
can offer.

Beyond fixes, ask broader questions
about help. If you have a problem with the
system, is there someone you can turn to
for advice? Do you have to pay for this
support, and when is it available?

Of course, not all CMSs come with
support. It's unusual for anything but
enterprise-level systems to offer this option.
If support isn't available, look at whether
the system has a vibrant community.

Community

The community is made up of individuals
who use the CMS. They share advice and
experiences via forums, mailing lists, and
support sites. Such communities are particularly important for open-source CMSs
because these products rarely offer formal
support and training. But many commercial
products also have excellent online communities.

If you encounter a problem with your
CMS outside of business hours, will you
be able to get help?

A good community can answer questions, offer support, and make available a range
of plug-ins you can use with your CMS. Before investing in a CMS, ensure that it has
a vibrant community. Visit the support site, and look at how many users are registered
and how often they post. Examine the topics people are discussing and particularly
how supportive they are to new users. It isn't unusual to find apparently vibrant
communities that are hostile to new users asking "dumb questions."

Next actions

This chapter has provided all the techniques you need to narrow down the thousands of CMSs to a handful of options. But you must make a final selection and implement your choice. This can be achieved in the following steps:

ACTION 1: *Get familiar.* Although reading about a CMS is important, you must see the system in action and if possible have some hands-on time with it. If you're buying the CMS from a provider, ask them to set up a test installation so you can use the system yourself. If you're using an open-source program, try the online demonstration and watch any video tutorials they have. Do everything you can to become familiar with the system.

ACTION 2: *Collect references.* Unfortunately, no demonstration can tell you what a system will be like to use on a daily basis. Speak to existing customers. Ask them about their experiences of using the system and the installation process. Ask about the system's flexibility and ease of use. Bear in mind that nobody likes every aspect of their CMS.

ACTION 3: *Plan the implementation.* After you've made your selection, you need to set up your system. Don't underestimate this task. Not only does the system need to be installed and configured, but you also have to customize the templates and add your content. Work closely with your development team to establish schedules, and don't forget to leave adequate time for testing and bug fixing. Don't be surprised if it takes considerably longer than you expected.

One of the big problems you'll encounter when choosing a CMS is *technobabble*. Technobabble is the jargon thrown at you by developers when they talk about technology. The next chapter will help you decode this foreign language.

9

Decoding technobabble

In this chapter

W eb developers are precise people. They have to be, to explain complex concepts in a clear way to other developers. Inaccuracy and oversimplification cause mistakes and confusion.

Web developers are going to hate this chapter.

The problem is that they have developed their own vocabulary to explain these complex technologies and concepts. *AJAX*, *web services*, *XML*, *schemas*, *domains*, *client side*, *MYSQL…* the list of terms goes on. Although these terms are meaningful to web developers, they sound like technobabble to everybody else.

Web developers will hate this chapter because I oversimplify things to make them intelligible. As a result, some of what I explain will be only part of a larger picture. But it's more important to grasp the concepts than it is to understand the specifics. It's this compromise that many web developers fail to make.

In this chapter, I aim to decode the technobabble and explain how the web works, including concepts you need to understand like the peculiarities of browsers; terms like *client side*, *server side*, and *hosting*; and buzzwords like *AJAX* and *Web 2.0*.

Let's begin by looking at how the web works.

UNDERSTAND THE WEB

Although I'm using a word-processing program to write this book, I have little understanding of how it works. I have a vague notion that everything I type is somehow converted into ones and zeros, but I don't know how that happens. It feels like magic. To the majority of us, that is also how the web feels. We're happy to use it but have no idea how it works.

Fortunately, you don't need to know how the web works. That said, a basic understanding is useful for those times when the web doesn't behave as expected. At least then you'll understand why it's causing you problems.

How are you able to open web browser and almost instantly find out anything?

To the majority of us, the web feels like magic. We have no idea how it works.

Moving data from the web to your desktop

Most of us know that the web consists of a vast network of computers spread across the globe. Although that is the extent of our knowledge, it's also a fairly accurate description. But knowing more will help explain why sometimes users can't see your website.

Most people connect to the web through a telephone line. The speed of this connection is dictated by the quality of the line. A growing number of users have access via cable. Either way, when a user requests a page from your site, the request doesn't go straight to the computer holding the page—first it's sent to an *internet service provider*.

The internet service provider (ISP) is the organization that you pay for web access. Hundreds of thousands of ISPs connect people to the web.

The primary job of the ISP is to pass a request for a page to the computer holding that page. It first needs to know where that computer is; and to find out, it needs to contact a *domain name server (DNS)*, which is effectively a photo book of IP addresses.

Every computer connected to the internet has a unique number that identifies it, called an *IP address*. Think of this as the computer's telephone number. Try opening a web browser and typing 12.129.147.65 into the address bar: you'll be taken to the Washington Post website.

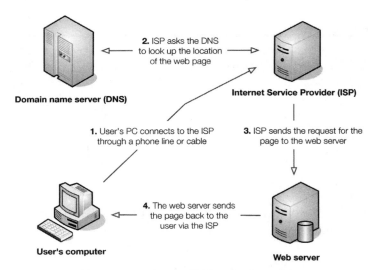

Domain name server (DNS)

2. ISP asks the DNS to look up the location of the web page

Internet Service Provider (ISP)

1. User's PC connects to the ISP through a phone line or cable

3. ISP sends the request for the page to the web server

4. The web server sends the page back to the user via the ISP

User's computer

Web server

Many steps are involved in downloading a web page.
Unfortunately, there are also many things that can go wrong.

IP addresses are hard to remember, so you normally type a domain name such as washingtonpost.com. The DNS is a computer that matches domain names with IP addresses. After it has converted the domain name (washingtonpost.com) to an IP address (12.129.147.65) and informed your ISP, the ISP sends your request for the web page to the web server.

The web server is the computer that holds your website. It isn't very different from your home computer; with the right software, it's possible to host a website on your home computer. When the web server receives a request from the user, it finds the specific page and passes all of its files to the user via their ISP. The web page then appears in the user's browser.

All of this happens in a few milliseconds. The request for a page and the page itself pass around the globe almost instantaneously, bridging oceans and crossing continents. It isn't surprising that there are occasional problems. Three of the most common issues are

> Domain-name redirection

> Connection issues

> Slow downloads

Let's look at why each occurs and what solutions exist (if any).

Why can't you see my site when I can?

When you first launch your website, some users may be unable to see it. If you had an existing site, users may see that instead. If this is your first site, they may see nothing at all. It's confusing because some will be able to see the new site but others won't.

This issue is caused by the DNSs I mentioned earlier. When a new website address is created, or that address is associated with a different web server, the DNSs need to be told. Until this happens, the website address won't be recognized by the DNS or will go to the wrong place.

Choosing a domain name

Here are five tips for selecting a domain name:

• *Avoid hyphenated names.* They're easy to forget and hard to read over the phone.

• *Check your spelling.* Avoid incorrect spellings like *digg* and *flickr*. Also watch out for national differences (*color* versus *colour*).

• *Be descriptive.* Use a name that describes what the site is about.

• *Be local.* Be sure you get the extension for your country (such as .fr).

• *Keep it simple.* Use addresses than are short and easy to remember.

With so many DNSs worldwide, this update can take time. Also, some DNSs can be updated before others. This is how some can see the new site while others can't.

Updating DNSs can take up to 72 hours, so patience is required. If your site needs to be live for a specific date, you must plan ahead. Speak to your development team, because they will have several solutions to this problem—but you need to inform them well in advance.

Domain name updates aren't the only reason users may not be able to connect to your website.

Why is my site down?

A common point of contention between website owners and developers is connectivity. The website owner receives complaints from people who can't access the website, and yet the developer claims the site is running smoothly.

Web server problems are the primary cause of connectivity issues. But there can be other causes. Gather as much information for your developer as possible when you receive complaints. Ask the user

It's possible for your website to be unavailable for one person but viewable by everybody else.

➤ Whether they can connect to other websites

➤ How long they've had the problem

➤ If they have been able to access the site from other computers.

> ➤ What browser they're using

> ➤ Whether they've received an error message

Connectivity problems can be caused by numerous factors beyond the control of your web team. There may be problems with the user's computer, their connection to the phone line, their ISP, or even with the web itself. For example, entire countries have gone offline because undersea cables were severed.

With enough information, the developer can ascertain where the problem lies and how best to solve it. But sometimes the problem isn't unavailability, but slow access.

Why is my site so slow?

The speed at which your website downloads is important. Users will look elsewhere if they find your site frustratingly slow. Download speed is dictated by two factors: the size of your web pages and the size of the user's connection to the web.

Unfortunately, you can't control the user's connection. What you *can* control is the size of your web pages.

Traditionally, web designers have focused on making web pages as small as possible, but this focus has slipped with the proliferation of broadband. Large images and video have made web pages more attractive but considerably larger. Although there are techniques to minimize the size of a web page, you may have to compromise your content if you know users have a slow connection.

Before adding multimedia content to your site, consider carefully whether your users will have sufficiently fast connections.

Usually, download speed isn't an issue these days; but if you're receiving complaints, you may have to cut back on video, audio, and imagery. You may also have to ask your developers to streamline their code.

You now know how a web page is delivered to a user; but how is it created in the first place?

Understanding how web pages are built

Web pages are essentially text files. They contain special HTML tags, but you can open them in a text editor and read them.

These text files sit on a web server within folders, just like the files on your computer. For example, the web address http://boagworld.com/podcast/index.html loads an HTML file called index from a folder called podcast on the web server with which the boagworld.com domain name is associated.

But things aren't always that simple. Many websites generate their pages dynamically using some form of content management system (CMS; as discussed in chapter 8, "Taking control"). These pages don't exist as files. Instead, they're built as requested, using a combination of a database and server-side code.

The majority of technobabble used by developers relates in some way to this dynamic generation of pages. Terms like *MYSQL*, *SQL Server*, *ASP*, *PHP*, and *ColdFusion* all refer to this process. To decode this technobabble, you need to understand the concept of databases and server-side code.

What is a database?

A *database* is a receptacle for holding information. It does this using tables, rows, and columns. If you've used Microsoft Access or Excel, you're already familiar with databases.

CMSs use a database to hold information about your site. Every title, keyword, or other piece of information on a specific web page is held in the database.

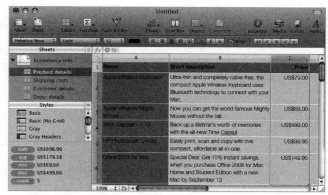

If you've used Numbers on the Mac or Excel on the PC, you have an idea of how a database works.

There are many different types of databases, from an Excel file to a massive Oracle database used on a heavily trafficked website. The majority of websites use either MYSQL or SQL Sever. The developer's choice is normally based on personal preference, restrictions of the web server, and which server-side language is being used.

What is a server-side language?

A *server-side language* is code that runs on the web server. This code can be written to fulfill a variety of tasks. The most common role is to extract content from a database and turn it into an HTML page. The code identifies the page the user wants, collects the appropriate information from the database, and turns this content into HTML before passing it back to the user.

You can choose from a variety of languages. Some of the most common are ASP, .NET, PHP, ColdFusion, Java, and Ruby. The pros and cons of these languages are beyond the scope of this book; it's a decision best left to the developer. As with databases, the

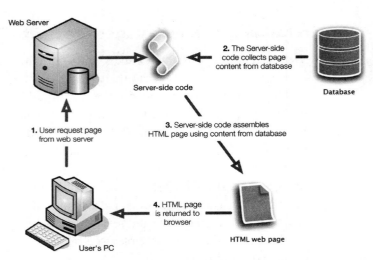

The most common function of server-side code is to extract content from a database and deliver it as HTML to the user's browser.

decision is based on personal preference and restrictions of the web server. But you must be aware of dangers during the selection process.

In chapter 8, I mentioned the danger of being tied to a particular developer because they chose to code in obscure language. I was talking about their choice of server-side language.

Ask your developer what server-side language they intend to use. If it's one I've named, then you're fine. If it isn't, ask around and see if other developers can support the language. Ask the developer why they chose it. If their answer doesn't make sense to you, ask for clarification. Some developers unintentionally use technobabble to avoid answering a question. Challenge them, even at the danger of looking stupid.

Today, the web model I outlined earlier is beginning to change. Content isn't always delivered as HTML, and the web is no longer just a series of pages being loaded. We're beginning to see the emergence of a new web: Web 2.0.

Understanding Web 2.0, AJAX, and other buzzwords

The term *Web 2.0* is in some senses a pointless buzzword that's often thrown around. But it's a term you may encounter, so it's worth addressing. There is little agreement as to the nature of Web 2.0. This term emerged to describe a subtle change in modern websites. I've seen *Web 2.0* used to describe the following:

> *A design aesthetic*—Web 2.0 sites often have a specific look and feel that uses large typography, color gradients, and reflections.

> *Open data*—Some Web 2.0 sites make their content available to desktop applications, web feeds, and other sites. This has led to a wealth of sites that combine content from other sites in innovative ways.

> *A community-led focus*—Web 2.0 sites usually have a community component. This can range from sites like YouTube that are entirely community driven to comments on a blog post.

> *A desktop-like experience*—Web 2.0 sites often use JavaScript to create a more desktop-like experience. This is achieved by reducing the number of page refreshes required through the use of AJAX.

AJAX uses JavaScript to grab content from the web and add it to existing pages without the need to refresh the page. This allows sites like Google Maps to constantly update content (in this case, a map) without waiting for the page to reload. It has become the basis for many web applications available today.

Asking for "a Web 2.0 site" is meaningless. Web 2.0 is a methodology, not a deliverable.

Google Maps uses JavaScript and AJAX to update maps without needing to reload the page.

Although impressive, this approach has drawbacks. AJAX can create accessibility problems for search-engine indexing, older browsers, and people using screen readers.

AJAX and Web 2.0 features are tools in your arsenal for creating a great website, but they aren't the final objective. Don't let them become a distraction. AJAX is heavily dependent on the browser—and as you'll discover, the browser is far from perfect.

GRAPPLE WITH THE BROWSER

The *browser* is a desktop application that displays web pages constructed from HTML, cascading stylesheets (CSS), and assets (video, images, and so on). It's what is referred to as a *client-side application*.

The client side is the user's PC. If the browser runs code it has downloaded, this is *client-side code*. Code that is running on the web server is *server-side code*. This includes the programming languages mentioned previously.

Although the server side (your web server) is a predictable environment, the client side (the browser) isn't. On the server side, you decide what technology is installed, how powerful the server is, and what the connection to the web is like. On the client side, you have no control. The unpredictability of the client side can lead to a plethora of problems, the greatest of which is the differences between browsers.

Mobileme as viewed in Safari

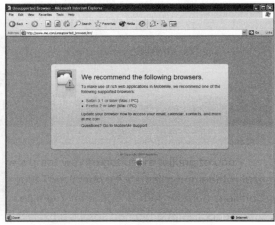

Mobileme as viewed in Internet Explorer 6

Internet Explorer 6 is less capable than modern browsers. Some organizations,
such as Apple, have decided to no longer support it, and others provide stripped-down sites.

Different browsers, different bugs

Gone are the days when a site could cater to almost all users by designing for Internet Explorer (IE). Users are increasingly adopting alternative browsers such as Firefox, Google Chrome, Opera, and Safari. By ignoring browsers other than IE, you potentially turn users away because your website doesn't appear consistently across browsers. Just because a website looks perfect in one browser doesn't mean it will look that good in every browser. Whether this is because of different interpretations of the HTML specification or bugs in the browser, sometimes a browser displays a page incorrectly.

To make matters worse, each browser has different versions. These can make a difference in the way they display pages. For example, IE 6 had a substantial number of misinterpretations of the HTML specification that caused all kinds of problems. Many of these problems were corrected in IE 7, but it broke sites that had been designed to work around the shortcomings in IE 6.

Many website owners become frustrated with their developers when their site doesn't display consistently across all browsers. They receive complaints from users and want to know why there are problems. In reality, it's inevitable. With a growing number of browsers and multiple versions of each, problems will occur.

The only solution to this problem is careful and systematic testing. When issues are identified, workarounds can be found and implemented. This is a time-consuming and expensive process. The more browsers you test, the more expensive it becomes.

Even the largest organization draws a line. Yahoo! is one of the biggest sites on the web, but it chooses not to test every browser variant. Instead, it has a process of *graded support*.

Caching conundrum

Imagine this scenario. You ask your designer to make a change to an image on your website. You check the site, and the change hasn't been made. When you confront the designer, they claim to have made the change, but you can't see it. The reason is that the browser has cached the image.

When you visit a web page, the browser stores a copy of that page for future use. This means the page loads faster when you return, because the browser doesn't have to download it again. Most of the time, this is hugely beneficial; but occasionally you see out-of-date content because the browser doesn't realize that things have changed.

Quick tip to avoid cached content

To make sure you're viewing the most up-to-date version of a page, hold down the Shift key when you click Refresh in your browser. Doing so forces the browser to download the latest version of the page.

	Win 2000	Win XP	Win Vista	Mac 10.4	Mac 10.5
Firefox 3.+	A-grade	A-grade	A-grade	A-grade	A-grade
Firefox 2.+		A-grade			A-grade
IE 7.0		A-grade	A-grade		
IE 6.0	A-grade	A-grade			
Opera 9.5 +		A-grade			A-grade
Safari 3.1 +				A-grade	A-grade

Yahoo! rates browsers by their capabilities and popularity. Capable, modern browsers (A-grade) are tested more thoroughly. For more information about this approach to browser support, visit http://developer.yahoo.com/yui/articles/gbs/.

Graded browser support doesn't attempt to provide the same visual experience to all browsers. It accepts that some browsers aren't capable of displaying modern websites or are too buggy to do so reliably. Instead, browsers are classified into categories and receive different visual appearances depending on that category. For example, A-grade browsers are modern browsers that are less buggy and more capable. These browsers receive the full visual experience and are carefully tested to ensure that they work correctly. C-grade browsers have limited functionality and so are given only a basic visual appearance. Some categories receive more testing than others depending on the level of usage they receive.

This approach can seem foreign to many website owners. They're used to print design, where everyone sees a brochure the same way. In chapter 4, "Differences over design," I explained how screen resolution and page constraints can alter the way a user sees a design. Well, the browser can, too. This is the nature of the web; and insisting on pixel-perfect design across every browser is not only unachievable but expensive.

Unfortunately, differences in user experience don't end with the browser. What the user sees is also affected by the plug-ins installed.

Plug-in problems

Browsers understand only a basic set of technology. They know how to display HTML and CSS. They can interpret JavaScript and a few other technologies, but that's about it. They aren't designed to handle video, games, or other multimedia elements. Today's rich internet experience is only possible because of plug-ins.

Plug-ins are essentially mini applications that can be added to a browser, enabling it to understand and run other technologies. The most widespread plug-in is the Flash player. Flash is a technology that lets web designers create complex animations, play video, and build desktop-like applications. Much of this would be extremely hard or impossible without a plug-in.

With plug-ins offering such a wealth of additional functionality, why do many web designers shy away from using them? The answer lies in their availability.

The problem with a plug-in is that the user is required to install it. Unfortunately, due to security concerns, browser manufacturers won't allow plug-ins to be automatically installed. Therefore, you have no guarantee that a specific plug-in will be present. Without that certainty, you must consider what will happen if it isn't there.

One approach is to ask the user to install it; but fears about spyware, viruses, and performance problems can make users reluctant. Some may be unable to install it due to corporate restrictions or lack of knowledge. You can't rely on users to install software.

You have two options to solve this problem. First, if the content isn't critical, you can hide it from users who don't have the plug-in. Second, if the content is critical, you must provide an alternative method of accessing it, as discussed in chapter 7, "Ensuring access for all." Producing content twice (once for the plug-in and once in an accessible form) is expensive and time consuming.

Sites like Vimeo and YouTube rely heavily on Flash to display animation. What happens when Flash isn't available?

Some say this problem doesn't apply to all plug-ins. Adobe argues that 99% of all users have Flash installed. If so many users have Flash, why worry about an alternative version? Here are three reasons:

> *Multiple versions*—Even though Flash is almost universally available, not everyone has the latest version. Like browsers, there are many different versions of most plug-ins, and the functionality supported by each version varies. Just because a user has the right plug-in doesn't mean they will be able to view your content.

> *Alternative devices*—High-penetration figures almost always refer to installations running on a PC. This doesn't take into account the growing number of users accessing the web via cell phones or other devices. For example, at the time of writing, the iPhone is unable to access content built in Flash. Content contained

in plug-ins is generally also inaccessible to users of screen readers and other assistive technologies.

> *Search-engine placement*—Most content designed for plug-ins is inaccessible to search engines. This has a significant effect on your site's ranking. Although some improvements are being made in the indexing of Flash, it's still far from being as indexable as HTML.

The market penetration of a plug-in is important especially when multiple plug-ins provide the same functionality. For example, a number of plug-ins provide video, including Flash, Quicktime, Windows Media, Real Player, and more. Market penetration can be the deciding factor when selecting a plug-in. That said, these figures don't tell the whole story.

Fortunately, the unpredictability of the client side isn't reflected on the server. This brings us to hosting your website.

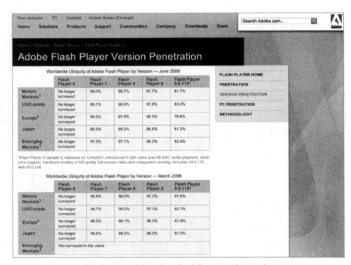

Adobe provides detailed figures about the penetration of its Flash plug-in.

HOST YOUR SITE

Choosing where to host your website can be confusing. You run the danger of paying too much, suffering from site outages, or even being unable to host your site at all. There is an overwhelming number of hosting companies (not to mention the possibility of hosting the site yourself) with countless ways to set up and run your website. You first need to narrow the field by clearly defining your requirements.

Assessing server requirements

The code written by your web developers may not run on your web server. That is why many website owners choose to have the web developers arrange hosting. If things don't work, you have only one person to blame! But that isn't always the right move. If you're using an external agency, they may charge a premium to host your site. Also, their package may not be as good as that offered by an independent supplier. Finally, you may already have a web server that would
be suitable for hosting. For any number of reasons, you may choose to organize things yourself.

If you wish to arrange hosting and want to avoid the scenario where your site doesn't work, then you need to know what code can or can't run on your web server.

Earlier, I explained that a web server uses databases and server-side languages to generate HTML for the browser. But a web server doesn't magically know how to run server-side code or access a database. You need to install software on the web server first. Without the right software, the server can't run the code that generates your website.

Two approaches will ensure that your web server and code are compatible. The first is the approach I proposed in chapter 3, "The perfect team," where you inform the developers about any technical constraints they have to work within. This now includes the limitations of your web server and which databases and server-side languages it can run. The alternative is to look for a hosting environment that supports the code produced by your developers.

LATE ON A FRIDAY...

AFTER 45 MINUTES ON HOLD WITH THE HOSTING COMPANY...

Website owners often let their developers arrange hosting so they have a single point of contact if things go wrong.

Compare Hosting Packages

Below is a feature comparison for all shared hosting packages.

Resource	Basic	Pro	Ultimate	Bus Basic	Bus Pro	Bus Advanced	Developer
Disk Space	1Gb	1.5Gb	2Gb	1Gb	2Gb	4Gb	1Gb
Bandwidth	20Gb	40Gb	75Gb	20Gb	40Gb	75Gb	10Gb
Websites	1	2	3	3	5	10	5
Subdomains	1	5	10	5	10	15	5
POP3 Accounts	3	7	10	10	20	30	5
FTP Accounts	1	2	3	3	5	10	3
SmarterStats Statistics	0	0	0	1	2	3	0
MySQL Databases	0	2	3	0	3	5	4
Microsoft SQL Databases	0	0	1	0	0	1	4
DNS Zone Editor	✗	✓	✓	✗	✓	✓	✓
ASP.NET 1.1 / 2.0 / 3.5	✗	✓	✓	✗	✓	✓	✓
ASP.NET AJAX 1.0	✗	✓	✓	✗	✓	✓	✓
ISAPI_Rewrite v3	✓	✓	✓	✓	✓	✓	✓
HotlinkBlocker	✓	✓	✓	✓	✓	✓	✓
ODBC DSN	0	2	4	1	5	10	10
Online file manager	✓	✓	✓	✓	✓	✓	✓
Standard Support	✓	✓	✓	✓	✓	✓	✓
Business Support	✗	✗	✗	✓	✓	✓	✗
Premium Support	✗	✗	✗	✗	✗	✗	✗
Uptime Guarantee	99.9%	99.9%	99.9%	99.95%	99.95%	99.95%	99.9%
Setup Fee	FREE	FREE	FREE	FREE	FREE	FREE	FREE
Yearly	£29.99	£39.99	£59.99	£109.99	£164.99	£249.99	£49.99
or Monthly		£3.99	£5.99	£10.00	£15.00	£25.00	£4.99
	Order	Order	Order	Order	Order	Order	Order

Many hosting companies offer a terrifying variety of hosting packages.

Your choice is largely dictated by circumstances. If you have an existing hosting environment, the developers must work within those constraints. If you don't, it's better to let the developer find hosting that fits their requirements. The next step is finding a hosting package that supports the server-side code you wish to run.

Finding the right hosting package

All you need to host your own website is a connection to the internet and a computer with the right software installed. This can be a cheap solution for those with low-traffic websites and the technical know-how to set up the server. Self-hosting is normally undertaken by large organizations that want to cut the cost of external hosting and have a lot of control over their sites.

For the vast majority, self-hosting isn't the best option. It requires a lot of technical support and can become expensive if you have to scale your hosting to support a popular site. Most sites therefore sign up for a hosting package with an external company.

Every provider has a variety of packages to accommodate different configurations. At the most basic level, you have two choices: dedicated or shared hosting. Your web developers should advise you about the appropriate solution for your site. But because your choice has business ramifications, you need to understand the options. Let's start with shared hosting.

Shared hosting

With shared hosting, your site shares the same web server with a number of other sites. The advantage is that you also share the cost of the server. Shared hosting tends to be significantly cheaper than dedicated hosting, which is why it tends to be the most popular solution for small to medium-size businesses.

Shared hosting has its drawbacks. You're limited to a set of preinstalled software that comes with your hosting plan. If you're using a popular server-side language and a common database, this won't be a problem—you buy hosting that includes the combination of software you

Although shared hosting is adequate for most websites, you may encounter performance issues.

need. But if your configuration is unusual, you may struggle to find appropriate hosting. Shared hosting can also be a problem if you add functionality in the future. If you introduce functionality that uses different technology, it may be necessary to change your hosting package in order to install that technology.

Fortunately, these restrictions are beginning to change. Options are now available that give you the same level of control as a dedicated solution. But they're harder to find, they're more expensive, and they suffer from the next issue: performance.

Because you share your web server with others, there is a danger that those sites may affect the speed of yours. For example, if the other sites are badly coded, they can cause the whole server to run slowly. Another possibility is that somebody's site may experience an increase in traffic, causing the web server to work harder delivering the new page requests.

Most shared web servers are capable of dealing with these problems, and hosting companies monitor performance carefully. Shared hosting is adequate in most situations; but if you require more control, consider dedicated hosting.

Dedicated hosting

With dedicated hosting, you buy or rent a web server that resides at a hosting company. It's like hosting the site yourself, but the server resides at a professional data center. The advantages are better security (important for storing personal information) and a faster web connection.

Dedicated hosting also avoids the problems of shared hosting. Because only your site resides on the server, there are no performance issues caused by other sites. You also have complete access to the computer, so you can install any software you choose.

Media Temple is one of a growing number of hosting companies to offer dedicated virtual hosting. This is shared hosting that has many of the benefits of dedicated hosting, including the ability to install whatever software you wish.

The downside is price. Dedicated hosting is expensive compared to shared. You must consider the cost of hosting and the additional expense of associated software, which can range from free (for open source solutions) to thousands of dollars for enterprise-level applications. That said, the cost of dedicated hosting is coming down, and some excellent deals are available. Dedicated hosting remains the best option for highly trafficked websites, those that require custom-installed software, and organizations running a number of different sites.

Deciding on the type of hosting and what software you require will go a long way toward narrowing the field. Just as when you're selecting a CMS, you must also consider the company behind the product. In this case, you need to assess the hosting provider.

Assessing hosting companies

Assuming that your site doesn't require anything unusual in terms of hosting, you'll be faced with a plethora of potential providers. Some will be temptingly cheap, but be wary of buying on price alone. You should consider a number of other criteria:

> Uptime

> Support

> The control panel

> Limitations on growth

> Hidden charges

Let's look at each, starting with uptime.

Uptime

The last thing any website owner wants is for their website to be unavailable. Many hosting companies therefore provide uptime guarantees.

Most uptime guarantees are worthless. The figures quoted are merely goals the company is striving for.

Figures range from 95% uptime to 100%. What exactly are they guaranteeing, and is it something you should worry about?

In most cases, uptime guarantees are worthless. They don't guarantee that your website will be available 100% of the time—that's merely a figure the hosting company is striving for. If they fail, they will compensate you. This compensation usually involves a partial refund of your hosting bill, but it could be insignificant compared to the losses in sales during downtime. Always clarify what compensation is being offered.

Remember that even the largest organizations have downtime. It's a problem that can never be entirely avoided. Websites may be unavailable due to connectivity issues, poor code, or any number of reasons beyond the control of your hosting company. As a result, such companies often specify exclusions from compensation in their terms of service.

In short, uptime guarantees are nothing but marketing tools. Instead of focusing on a guarantee, search for reviews of the hosting company or look at their support forum. If you see lots of complaints about downtime, think twice. But in most cases, the service offered in regard to uptime is fairly universal.

Instead of asking how often your site is likely to go down, ask what will happen when it does. What kind of support can you expect?

Support

Support is arguably the single most important factor in choosing a hosting company. Whether it's your website going offline or a piece of functionality not running, you'll inevitably have problems with your hosting. When that happens, you need to quickly reach somebody who can help.

How can you tell if a hosting company offers good support? Look for the following things:

When your website goes offline, you want to be sure of a fast response.

> ➤ *24/7/365 support*—When your website is offline, you need to be able to get help instantly. Check that your hosting company offers support 24 hours a day, 7 days a week, 365 days a year.

> ➤ *Telephone support*—There is an increasing trend toward email-only support. But technical problems can be hard to diagnose, and prolonged conversation via email is time consuming. When your site is offline, you need the immediacy of a phone call. Be sure that option is available to you.

> *Speedy response*—Whether you're contacting your hosting company by email or phone, you should expect a speedy response. It's unacceptable to sit on hold while your site is down or wait days for a response to an email query. I recommend calling the technical support telephone number before you sign up for service. How long do you have to wait before speaking to a real human being? Also, send a question via email and see how long it takes to get a reply.

> *In-country support*—Personally, I prefer speaking to local support staff. Being put through to call centers in far-flung locations can be frustrating when you're discussing complex technical problems. If you don't share the first language of support staff, misunderstandings can occur more easily. By calling the support number before signing up, you can establish whether you will have communication problems.

> *Knowledgeable staff*—Call centers are often manned by individuals with limited technical knowledge. This can be frustrating when you're endeavoring to resolve technical issues. Ideally, you should be able to speak directly to the individuals managing the web servers. If you aren't a technical person, ask your web developers to speak to the support staff at the hosting company before signing up. They should be able to judge the staff's technical competency.

> *Technobabble-free support*—Talking to support staff can be equally frustrating if they're overly technical. By calling the support line before purchasing, you should be able to get a sense of their communication skills.

> *Self-service support*—Contacting technical support is the last resort. In most cases, you should be able to find the answer to questions through your hosting company's support site. Look at their site and see if they have frequently asked questions, a knowledge base, forums, and a list of current known issues. Facilities like this can save you time, so be sure they're available.

Self service should also extend beyond support. Most hosting companies provide a control panel for managing your site.

The control panel

Calling technical support every time you want to change a password is frustrating, so most hosting companies provide a control panel for basic maintenance. This includes managing email, changing passwords, uploading files, performing backups, and accessing site statistics.

A web-based control panel allows you to carry out basic maintenance on your site.

Evaluate the control panel, and discuss it with your developers. If the hosting company doesn't have a demo available on the site, call and ask for access to one. If nothing else, this will demonstrate how responsive their customer service is.

When you have access, ask yourself whether it provides all the functionality you require. Is it easy to understand and use? For example, how does it handle the management of multiple sites? This is particularly important as your online presence grows.

Limitations on growth

As your site becomes more successful, you'll become more ambitious in your plans, and visitors will flock to your site in ever larger numbers. Will your hosting company keep up with this growth? To answer this question, you need to know the answers to the following three questions:

> *Can you manage multiple websites centrally?* You may start with a single site; but if it's a success, you may want to launch more, such as a subsite that supports a marketing campaign or a site dedicated to a subset of your audience. These sites need to be managed centrally, so avoid multiple logins to administer multiple sites. Check with your hosting company to be sure they provide a single interface to manage multiple sites.

> *What is the upgrade path?* As your site grows in terms of visitors and complexity, you may need to migrate from shared hosting to dedicated hosting. You may even need to upgrade your dedicated box to something more powerful. It's important to understand how this process works. You want to avoid the need to back up your entire site and reinstall it. A good hosting company should make this a seamless transition.

> *What happens if you exceed your bandwidth limits?* The more successful your website, the more expensive it will be in terms of bandwidth. Most hosting plans come with a bandwidth limit. The hosting company has to pay for each

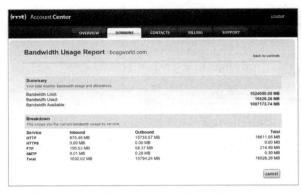

If your hosting plan has a bandwidth limit, does your control panel display current bandwidth usage?

piece of data a user downloads from your site, so it caps how much data it allows to be downloaded. The cap is more than adequate for most sites, but what happens if you exceed your bandwidth limit? How much extra will it cost? What happens if you exceed your limit without a higher-rate package in place? Will it costs you even more? Does the control panel provide a way to monitor current bandwidth use?

Bandwidth isn't the only thing that can become expensive. You may discover other hidden charges, too.

Hidden charges

Some hosting companies appear to be inexpensive on the surface but then hit you with hidden costs. Establish what is included in the monthly charge and what isn't. I've encountered hosting companies that charged extra for the following:

> More than a predefined number of email accounts

> Advanced email functionality, such as Exchange server or spam filters

> A technician to physically restart your web server

> Add-on technologies

> The ability to run databases

> Access to website statistics

Establish what is included in your monthly charge to help avoid hidden charges. Additional bandwidth usage is just one hidden cost that may show up on your bill.

The list could go on. There is nothing wrong with hosting companies using this form of modular pricing; it can keep the price down if you require only basic functionality. The problem comes when the hosting company doesn't clearly communicate these additional costs and they come as a surprise.

Next actions

Commissioning a website is a mine field of jargon and technical detail. This chapter has tackled the key technical issues you need to know. We've addressed how the web works and why things sometimes go wrong. We've looked at how web pages are created and how that process is changing thanks to AJAX. We've also investigated potential problems with browsers and, most important, looked at how you host your site.

Now it's time to turn what you've learned into action:

ACTION 1: *End the technobabble.* Stop allowing your developer to use language you don't understand. Next time they do, ask them to explain. It's their responsibility to ensure that you have the information you require to make informed decisions. You shouldn't be embarrassed to ask if you don't understand something.

ACTION 2: *Choose a host.* If you have yet to arrange hosting, now is the time to speak to your developer using the knowledge from this chapter. Together, you can investigate the options available. Alternatively, if you already have hosting, begin a review of the service. Does it measure up to the criteria we've discussed? Should you consider alternatives?

ACTION 3: *Expand your vocabulary.* I've only scratched the surface of the technobabble you may encounter. If you come across terminology and can't get an explanation, I recommend looking the glossary of terms found on the Sitepoint website (http://sitepoint.com/glossary/). It provides definitions for everything from *access keys* to *XHTML*.

You now have all the information you need to commission and build a website. We've addressed writing a brief; assembling your team; designing your site; writing content; and ensuring usability, accessibility, and best practice. We've even looked at how to find a host for your site.

Does that mean your job is done? Unfortunately not. Although the build phase is over, you still need to promote your site, engage with your users, and plan for the future. We'll address this next, starting with site promotion.

10

Driving traffic

In this chapter

In the movie *Field of Dreams*, Kevin Costner hears a voice in his corn field tell him, "If you build it, he will come." Many website owners have this mentality: they believe that if they build a website, users will turn up. They mistakenly see their website as a marketing tool in its own right. Unfortunately, it doesn't work like that.

The best way to think of a website is as a store front. If you open a new store, a few people will wander in, but they won't come in substantial numbers. To make your shop a success, you need to promote it.

You must continually promote your site if you want to maintain a high level of new visitors. It isn't enough to promote your site when it's first launched. A long-term strategy for site promotion is required.

Many website owner see search-engine placement as the answer for their long-term strategy. They spend vast amounts of money on search-engine optimization experts. But search-engine placement is only a single component in a larger strategy. You also need to actively pursue your audience, create great content, and promote your site offline.

Nevertheless, being ranked well on sites like Google is the linchpin of your broader strategy. We'll begin by looking at the role of the search engine.

BECOME NUMBER 1 ON GOOGLE

My publisher will love the fact that I have a section entitled "Become number 1 on Google." Titles like that sell books. After all, that is what every website owner wants.

There is no shortage of companies promising the number-1 position. But can they really deliver what they offer? To answer that question, I need to refer back to something I said in chapter 7, "Ensuring access for all": "Search engines are interested in only one thing: providing relevant results to their users."

If your content isn't relevant, no amount of clever search-engine optimization will get you to number 1.

Car manufacturer BMW was effectively removed from the Google search engine after attempting to inappropriately manipulate its ranking.

There are ways to trick Google into ranking your site better, but these break Google's guidelines. Search-engine optimization (SEO) companies sometimes use these techniques to improve rankings. In almost all cases, the benefit is temporary, because Google works to close such loopholes.

Google comes down hard on sites that disregard the guidelines, but techniques are available to legitimately improve your ranking. These focus on removing obstacles that can hinder search engines from indexing the content of your site.

How can you distinguish between agencies that use legitimate techniques and those using black-hat techniques?

Avoiding being blacklisted

Although many companies provide valuable SEO services, a number are out to deceive. You can identify a less-than-reputable SEO company by looking at two things: information about the company and the techniques they choose to use. Let's address each in turn.

Spotting black-hat operators

Be skeptical of any company that contacts you out of the blue. The ideal way to find an SEO company is via personal recommendation. Failing that, apply the same methodology you used to select a web-design company in chapter 2, "Stress-free planning."

Beware of companies that guarantee a particular ranking. If a company promises that you'll be ranked number 1 on Google, ask for more information. It's easy to be ranked number 1 on Google for an obscure term; it's much harder for something that is useful from a marketing perspective.

What happens if a company fails to live up to its guarantee? Is there any real value in their promise? Probably not.

Ask the SEO company to clearly explain the techniques it uses. Don't use a company that's evasive in answering this question. If you discover the techniques the company intends to implement, you can judge whether you're in danger of being blacklisted.

Spotting black-hat techniques

Google provides excellent documentation on how to improve your ranking. It also provides advice about avoiding unacceptable SEO techniques. These nefarious techniques include the following:

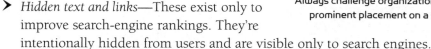

Always challenge organizations that guarantee prominent placement on a search engine.

> *Hidden text and links*—These exist only to improve search-engine rankings. They're intentionally hidden from users and are visible only to search engines.

> *Search-engine-only content*—Using techniques such as redirects and cloaking, it's possible to present different content to a search engine than to a real user. This approach is often used by sites built in Adobe Flash, because search engines find it hard to index Flash sites. This breaks Google's terms of service.

> *Automatically submitting to Google*—Many SEO companies use software packages such as Web Position to automatically submit websites to multiple search engines. This is specifically prohibited by Google's terms of service.

> *Duplicating content*—Although Google recognizes that some content can be duplicated for legitimate reasons (such as a separate print version of your site), it frowns on websites that are deliberately duplicated in an attempt to manipulate rankings.

> *Doorway pages*—These pages are created with the sole purpose of ranking well for certain keywords. They often have poor content and exist solely to funnel users to the main site.

> *Keyword stuffing*—This is the practice of loading a webpage with keywords in an attempt to manipulate rankings. This creates a negative user experience and may ultimately cause Google to take action.

> *Participating in link schemes*—Although site ranking is partially based on who links to you, link-exchange programs are a bad idea. Exchanging links without considering their relevancy will damage your ranking.

The BMW website presented different content to users (top) than it did to search engines (bottom). This broke Google's guidelines for webmasters.

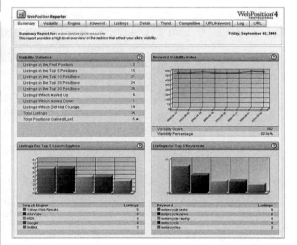

WebPosition (http://www.webposition.com/) is one of many tools that will automatically submit your site to search engines. Although these tools save time, they break Google's terms of service.

Will implementing these techniques get you removed from Google? Probably not. But they will damage your ranking over the long term and almost certainly be a waste of money.

Should you therefore avoid hiring SEO companies? Not necessarily. Many reputable companies offer superb advice about how to improve your rankings. Use what you've learned here to find a respectable supplier.

But what if you can't afford a SEO expert? What can you do yourself?

Improving your search-engine ranking

You and your team can do a number of things to improve your placement on search engines. These fall into three broad categories:

> Improving your site's build

> Improving your site's content

> Encouraging quality links

We've touched on the subject of building for search engines in chapter 7, but there is more you can do.

Improving your site's build

In chapter 7, you learned how accessibility can improve search-engine placement. You know to avoid content types that search engines can't access (like Adobe Flash), and you understand how to mark up content semantically and use appropriate **ALT** and **TITLE** attributes. Although these techniques ensure that content is accessible to search engines, it doesn't mean search engines will discover

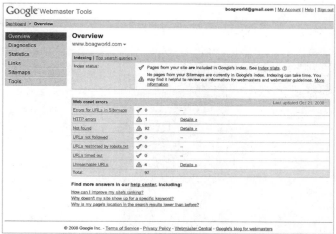

Google has a suite of tools that provides a way to make your site more Google-friendly. They show you Google's view of your site, help you diagnose problems, and let you share information with Google to improve your site's visibility.

that content in the first place. The following techniques can help ensure that Google and other search engines discover your content:

> *Create a clear hierarchy.* Every page should be reachable from at least one other page of your site.

> *Use text links.* Links between pages should be textual rather than use images, Flash, or other inaccessible technologies.

> *Use short URLs.* Some web addresses created by dynamically driven websites (such as those built using content management systems) cause problems for search engines. Shorter web addresses that are easy to read by a person and use fewer parameters (characters after the ? in the address) are more likely to be found.

> *Add a site map.* Add a site map that includes links to important content. Try not to exceed 100 links on a page, because doing so can cause problems.

> *Submit your site.* A search engine finds your site through those who link to you. Speed up the process by submitting your site for indexing. For Google, you can do this at http://www.google.com/addurl.html. You can also submit a site map using Google's webmaster tools. Doing so helps Google learn the structure of your site and increases the number of pages indexed.

Now that search engines can access your website, you need to address the content.

Check that search engines can view your site using a text browser such as Lynx. Like Lynx, search engines are only interested in the textual content of your site.

Improving your site's content

The most important consideration when you're writing copy for search engines is the inclusion of search terms. Before you write a page, have a clear idea what it's about and what search terms people may use to find that subject. Next, incorporate them *naturally* into copy, headings, image **ALT** attributes, and the page title.

Be careful not to use too many search terms. Two or three per page is adequate. If you use more, the copy may become hard to read, and the ranking of each individual term will be reduced. Don't stuff a page with search terms, because you may be penalized for doing so. They should be incorporated naturally into your copy. Try reading your copy out loud—if it sounds like you're forcing the use of keywords, it requires some rewriting.

Focus on writing good copy. Well-written and engaging copy also attracts links.

Encouraging quality links

If you already run a website, you've probably received an email from somebody wanting to exchange links. The email may have explained that Google ranks pages by the number of incoming links. There is some truth in this claim: Google does *partially* rank pages based on the number of sites that link to yours. This isn't the whole story.

In reality, nobody but Google knows how it ranks sites. Links

Linking to sites that aren't relevant to your subject matter rarely provides SEO benefits.

are a factor, but more than the quantity matters. Google states, "The quantity, quality, and relevance of links count towards your rating."

Google looks at a number of factors:

> The subject matter of the linking site

> The copy that appears in the link

> The popularity of the linking site

> The reputation of the linking site

It's rarely worthwhile responding to a link request unless it comes from a high-profile website with appropriate content. But it's worth seeking links from relevant sites. Which sites would you like to appear on, regardless of the benefits to your ranking? Which sites does your target audience frequent? Getting featured on such sites provides benefits of its own. Later in the chapter, we'll discuss ways to be featured on these sites.

Although these techniques we've discussed will help improve your ranking, search engines shouldn't be your sole focus. Search engines have a lot of drawbacks.

Understanding the problem with search engines

Search engines aren't the most effective marketing tool. If it weren't for the large number of users they can potentially reach, I doubt website owners would invest time in gaining high placement on them.

Their unpredictable nature is frustrating. You can spend time and money refining keywords and optimizing pages, only to receive a poor ranking. There are no guarantees in SEO, and that is unusual for a marketing tool—for example, you wouldn't buy advertising in a newspaper without knowing how prominently your advertisement would appear. In addition, SEO isn't a one-time cost. With new sites coming online every day and existing sites jostling for position, maintaining your ranking is a continual battle.

SEO also raises usability concerns. The more you focus on search-engine rankings, the less you're focusing on users' needs. This can lead to your copy and navigation becoming stuffed with keywords and being hard to read.

To justify this aggravation, you would expect search engines to be a remarkable marketing tool. But SEO is a passive form of marketing. It relies on users' recognizing their need for a product or service. Unless they're aware of that need, they won't search for it and discover your site. Other forms of marketing both fulfill and *create* need. In this regard, search engines are weak.

They also rely on users typing in keywords you've included in your site. Unfortunately, people are unpredictable and may enter keywords you don't expect. Part of the problem is that we've all worked in our respective industries too long and use jargon unfamiliar to our users. Despite our best efforts, we lose potential visitors because they use different search phrases.

You wouldn't buy an ad in a newspaper without knowing where it will appear; but when you spend money on SEO, you have no guarantee where you'll be listed.

It can take months for a site to become listed and almost as long for SEO work to take effect. This makes it hard to tweak and improve your marketing campaigns. It also means that sites with short life spans (such as those for events) may not appear at all.

Despite all these frustrations, search engines can't be ignored. One way to relieve the pain is to use pay-per-click advertising.

Using pay-per-click advertising

Google Adwords are small text ads that appear above or to the right of search results on Google.

A number of organizations offer pay-per-click advertising, but Google Adwords dominates. Adwords appear on Google's search results and thousands of other websites. Any website owner can add them to a site as a way of generating income.

The ads consist of a short title, a two-line description, and a link. Each is associated with a set of keywords. The ad is displayed when a user searches for an associated keyword or visits a site that has Google ads and is considered relevant.

Ads are paid for on a per-click basis. You only pay when the ad is clicked and the user visits your site. The amount you pay depends on the popularity of the keyword entered by the user.

Although Google search results can display many ads, the top three slots are more likely to be clicked, and competition can be fierce. The more you're willing to pay, the higher your ad appears. Each advertiser specifies a maximum they're willing to pay per click, and the system ranks the advertisements accordingly.

Depending on the level of competition, you may be charged less than your maximum bid. You can further limit your spending by setting a daily budget. When this limit has been reached, your ad is removed.

With prices starting as low as 10c per click, and given the ability to control precisely your spending, Adwords is an attractive method of advertising. It also overcomes the limitations of normal search-engine listings:

> You have guaranteed placement.

> No adjustment to your site is required, thereby avoiding usability concerns.

> Return on investment is much more predictable.

> Your ad appears in a matter of minutes.

> You can target non-relevant keywords if you wish to create a need that doesn't currently exist.

Getting started with Adwords is easy, but mastering it requires some experimentation. Although it will drive traffic to your site immediately, you may overpay for each click initially, and the quality of traffic could be poor.

A common mistake is targeting broad keywords such as *men's fashion*. Competition for broad keywords is fierce, and prices are high. Broad keywords also generate lower-quality leads; those responding to ads on broad keywords are less likely to want your product. Instead, be specific with your keyword phrases. Instead of *men's fashion*, use multiple keywords that name specific brands.

Broad keywords are just one of the many mistakes first-time advertisers make. Read the help section on Google Adwords; it provides advice on selecting keywords, writing an effective ad, optimizing conversions, and tracking performance. It also offers several tools to help you run a campaign, like the keyword suggestion engine.

So far, this chapter has focused exclusively on search engines. But search engines are only a small part of your site's marketing strategy. What makes up the rest?

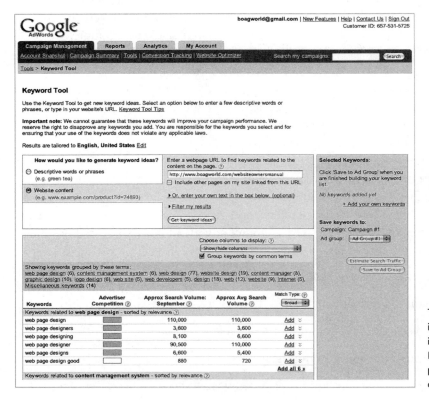

The Google keyword tool is invaluable when you're selecting keywords for your campaign. It makes suggestions based on phrases you enter or using the content of your website.

GO BEYOND THE SEARCH ENGINE

The opportunities for promoting your website are endless. With so many options, you must decide which approach is right for your site. This depends on your audience and objectives. But all websites should consider these three strategies:

A three-pronged marketing attack

Offline promotion

Audience targeting

Viral marketing

Each approach has pros and cons, but most campaigns incorporate them all to some extent. Let's begin by examining the most neglected of the three: offline promotion.

Offline promotion

It's amazingly easy to overlook the obvious. This is especially true for website owners, who spend so much time focusing on the web. They eventually develop tunnel vision when it comes to marketing. In their haste to improve search-engine rankings or get on Facebook, they overlook offline methods of promoting their sites, even though offline promotion can be powerful in certain circumstances. It's particular effective when you're trying to do the following:

> Reach an audience in a specific geographical area

> Encourage repeat traffic from existing customers

> Move customer interactions online

If you use any of the following forms of communication, they should also promote your website:

> Business stationery

> Traditional media

> Miscellaneous marketing material

> Word of mouth

The most obvious of these is business stationery.

When you're promoting your website offline, always place your website address alongside your logo.

Business stationery

A good rule of thumb when promoting your website offline is to place your website address wherever your logo appears. Nowhere is this more true than with business stationery. Business stationery includes business cards, letterheads, envelopes, leaflets, brochures, and any other form of documentation or paper-based promotional material. If you have a marketing style guide, amend it to mention the inclusion of your website address whenever possible.

You also have opportunities to promote your site in more overt traditional advertising.

Dell's TV ads encourage viewers to visit a specific page on the company's site. This page builds on the messages communicated in the TV spot.

Traditional media

In 2001, I worked for an internet startup that had raised significant capital through IPO. Flush with newfound wealth, it embarked on an aggressive marketing campaign developed by a top London advertising agency.

The first fruit of this campaign was a nationwide radio ad. Although it communicated our offering clearly, it failed to mention the website address!

Things have come a long way since 2001, but I still see organizations missing the opportunity to promote their websites in TV, radio, and newspaper ads. A website can be the perfect call to action that many ads lack.

Consider how you can tie the web and traditional media together. How can your site support your advertising and vice versa?

Although business stationery and traditional media encompass the majority of marketing opportunities for your website, you also have a plethora of other, smaller opportunities.

Miscellaneous marketing materials

Your branding appears on a host of items including company vehicles, uniforms, conference stands, and point-of-sale materials. There is also the marketing collateral many companies give away, including t-shirts, pens, mouse pads, calendars, and an abundance of other miscellaneous items.

These are all opportunities to put your website in front of potential customers. And one more means of offline promotion is often overlooked: word of mouth.

Word of mouth

Word of mouth is an effective means of promoting your site, and it begins with you. You need to convince your colleagues that your site has value and to spread the word.

Encourage your call center to point people at the website when possible. Sales people should use the website as part of their sales process. Even account managers, partners, and suppliers can refer people to the website.

You need to ensure that the site is a useful resource. If you followed my advice

Until you promote your website within your organization, staff won't tell customers about it.

in chapter 2, then you've spoken to internal stakeholders about how the site can be developed to accommodate their needs. Now you need to show them the benefits and encourage them to tell others.

Consider offering staff training or throwing a launch party when the site goes live. Send out a regular newsletter to employees, telling them about new site features. Maybe even make everybody's browser default to your home page. Anything to bring attention to the site.

Offline promotion needs to be accompanied by online marketing. You can do this using the scattershot approach of viral marketing or using a more targeted strategy.

Targeting your audience

One of my problems with search engines is that they're passive. They rely on users to recognize a need and actively look for it. Waiting for users to turn up isn't enough. You need to search them out and encourage them to visit your site.

You can actively pursue your target audience by frequenting websites they visit. These sites can be about anything, as long as they attract the right audience. For example, if you sell mobility scooters to the elderly, try looking on sites that cover retirement or health. Ask yourself what the audience is interested in, and find sites about that subject. When you've found some possible sites, identify the ones that offer promotional opportunities. You can use two types of sites this way:

> *Social*—Sites where your target audience meets to discuss common interests or share information

> *Editorial*—Sites that post articles, reviews, and other information appropriate to your target audience

You use these two types of sites in different ways. Get it wrong, and you can damage your brand and drive visitors away. This is especially true of social sites.

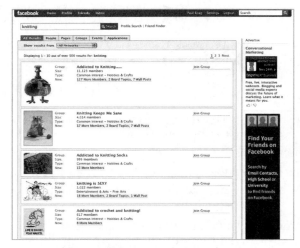

Facebook has groups catering to every possible interest. These groups can be an effective way of targeting your audience.

Social sites

Community websites are intrinsic to the web. They include forums, chat rooms, and mailing lists. Recently, the web has seen an explosion of community websites, serving every conceivable niche. From sites discussing politics or religion to hobbies such as knitting and hiking, the options are endless.

This explosion is partly due to sites like Facebook (http://facebook.com) that make it easy for anybody to create a community group online. Whatever your target audience, there will be a social site where they meet.

How do you promote your website through these social sites? The answer is, carefully! Increasingly, website owners are recognizing the marketing value of social sites and spamming them with blatant promotion. This only serves to anger users and damage the perception of your brand. To effectively market to a social site, a more subtle approach is required. Always adhere to the following guidelines:

> *Build a reputation.* Never just start shouting about your site. You must earn the right to promote it. People need to know and trust you. This involves a long-term commitment to that community.

> *Use your profile.* Most communities provide profile pages. These allow you to post basic information about yourself and link back to your site. Completing your profile shows other users you're committed to the community.

> *Don't self promote.* Never post about your site directly. Instead, add a small link at the bottom of your post in the form of a signature.

Shouting at people on the street isn't an effective way to promote your website. The same is true online. Never post blatant ads for your site on social websites.

> *Follow the rules.* Be sure to read and follow any community rules about self promotion, or risk being banned.

> *Contribute value.* Avoid posts that add no value. Posting "Yeah, I agree" or "Good point" followed by a link to your site is spam. Build respect by posting useful responses and contributing value to the discussion. When you've done that, people will be more responsive to what you have to say and more likely to visit your site.

> *Admit mistakes.* If you overstep the line and users complain, apologize quickly. Never become defensive and avoid confrontation.

> *Don't spam.* Never spam a community. Don't visit a community, post, and never return. Don't post repetitively and indiscriminately.

Marketing through social sites is a long-term commitment, but it's worth it. Because of the commitment, you'll be able to target only a small number of communities. This won't drive large amounts of traffic, but the quality of those users will be high. They will know and respect you. They will be interested to hear what you have to say. Social sites are an excellent marketing opportunity for organizations trying to sell high-value services. In such cases, the quality of the leads matters more than the quantity.

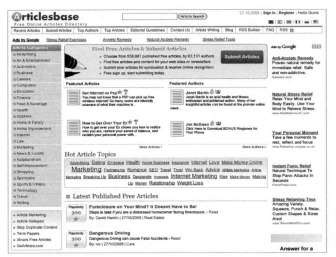

Sites like Articlesbase (http://articlesbase.com) distribute your articles for others to use. This can potentially lead to links back to your site. But a more effective approach is to contact specific sites that you would like to write for.

Social sites provide one promotional opportunity, but editorial sites allow for a different approach.

Editorial sites

Editorial sites are article based. They includes news, reviews, and magazine sites, as well as blogs. They tend to be topic oriented (such as sports) or lifestyle focused (like content for people over 50). Some are run by large professional organizations such as national newspapers; and others are run by enthusiastic amateurs, normally in the form of blogs.

Don't dismiss blogs. Some blogs have massive audiences that exceed those of traditional sites. Some blogs are highly influential and have a loyal subscriber base that takes the blogger's opinion seriously. These influential blogs are also monitored by mainstream media, which occasionally pick up their stories.

It can be tricky to get mentioned on these editorial sites. But you have three possible avenues:

> *Writing for them*—The best option is to write for these sites. They're always looking for content, and most are willing to consider submissions. When you submit articles, make sure they're relevant and interesting to the audience. Self promotion is unnecessary because the publisher normally links back to your site.

> *Commenting*—Many editorial sites allow readers to respond to an article in the comments. If you can't write for the site, begin posting comments on other articles they publish. As with social sites, it's easy to fall into the trap of spamming,

so make sure your comments add value and aren't self promotion. Comments let you add a link, so that is your opportunity to promote your site.

> *Emailing*—Email the publication and tell them about your site. Explain why the site is of interest to their audience, and suggest how they may wish to write about it. Provide a story or angle that the publication can write about.

Editorial sites are a highly targeted way of reaching users, but another approach can potentially drive many more users: viral marketing.

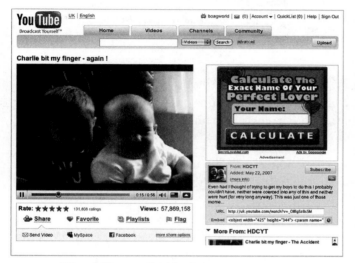

Although it's unpredictable, viral content can attract huge audiences. This video of a baby biting his brother's finger has been viewed 57 million times.

Viral marketing

Users turn to the web for entertainment as well as information. Sites like YouTube, Digg, Facebook, MySpace, and Twitter have exploded in popularity because they offer social interaction, amusing videos, and entertaining content. Content on these sites is user generated and gains popularity through peer-to-peer recommendation. If people like the content, they pass it on. *Going viral* can generate a lot of traffic.

Popular content on YouTube may be viewed by millions of users. And Digg has become known for the *digg effect*, where entire sites collapse under the weight of the traffic Digg sends. With the ability to generate high levels of traffic, viral marketing can appear appealing. But these figures can be misleading. The quality of traffic generated through viral marketing tends to be poor, for a number of reasons:

> *It's much harder to target specific audiences.* With viral marketing, you have little control over who is exposed to your content. Although the nature of the content has some influence, viral marketing isn't as refined as other methods.

> *Users don't care about your site.* Users are interested in the content of your viral marketing, not what your site can offer. This significantly reduces conversion.

Social news website Digg (http://digg.com) has gained a reputation for forcing websites offline because it can drive so much traffic to a site.

> *They're unlikely to remember you.* The typical user who views viral marketing sees a lot of similar content. Unless yours is exceptional, they're unlikely to remember you. Even if they do, they're more likely to remember the marketing rather than your site.

Does this mean you should avoid viral marketing? Not at all. If your campaign is successful, the large number of eyeballs will generate enough good leads to justify the investment.

Producing the kind of content that stands out is challenging. Unless you hire experts in viral marketing, it's a high-risk strategy with a low chance of success. Here are some tips that will give your campaign the best chance of going viral:

> *Aim to create a reaction.* Whether you shock or make people laugh out loud, it's important to get a reaction. If you don't, they won't pass your message on to a friend.

> *Be unexpected.* With so many funny videos and clever blog posts vying for attention, you need to stand out from the crowd. Be original.

> *Never sell directly.* People don't want an advertisement promoting your site. They want to be entertained or engaged. People don't pass on ads.

> *Enable passing.* Make it easy for users to share your campaign. If possible, let them customize or comment on it.

> *Utilize trends.* If something is cool or in the news, use it to your advantage. Build a campaign around what people are already talking about.

A case study in viral marketing: Dexter

An example of good viral marketing is for the TV show *Dexter*. Dexter follows the story of a mass-murdering vigilante. It's a quirky and sometimes humorous drama whose viral marketing campaign expertly picked up on this vibe.

The campaign lets you play a prank on friends using a personalized video. You enter a few basic details about your friend, including their name, occupation, and age. A link is sent to your friend, referring them to a spoof video news site. This includes a video of a police press conference about a serial killer. The police indicate that they have evidence identifying the next victim. They mention the victim's occupation, age, and other details that you entered earlier. It concludes with a piece of paper containing a series of crossed-out names and the name of your friend, implying that your friend is the next victim.

This campaign succeeded for a number of reasons. It was shocking and received national coverage. It was also funny for those in on the joke and easy to pass on, and nothing like it had been done before.

> *Follow up.* Viral marketing is pointless without a call to action. What is it, and what happens when people respond? Don't just send users to your home page. Consider something more tailored to the campaign to lead them into your site.

There are no guarantees with viral marketing, which makes it risky. But get it right, and the rewards can be considerable.

By combining the various promotional approaches we've discussed, it shouldn't be long before you're driving traffic to your site. But how do you know which campaigns are successful and whether your site is doing its job?

MEASURE SUCCESS

In chapter 2, I explained how you can use free web-log analyzers like Google Analytics to gather quantitative data about your existing website. But they can also do the following:

> Monitor your marketing efforts

> Find and resolve problems with your site

> Identify popular content

Why then do most website owners fail to follow their web stats regularly? One reason is that they're unsure what to look for and how to interpret the results.

The best approach is to identify what you want to learn and then find the tool that gives you this information. For example, one of your aims is to monitor

Monitoring website statistics can be confusing if you don't know what you're looking for.

marketing efforts. How can website statistics packages help you achieve that?

Monitoring marketing

In chapter 2, I suggested that you monitor the number of unique users, because this is a sign of healthy marketing initiatives. Note that I referred to *unique users* and not hits or page views. Contrary to some website owners' beliefs, these metrics aren't generally worth following. *Hits* refers to the number of individual files downloaded from the web server. Because a page may consist of many files (HTML, CSS, images), the hit count is unrepresentative. Page views aren't much better. Just because a user is viewing a lot of pages doesn't mean they're finding the information they require. It could mean they're lost.

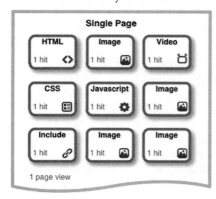

A single page may consist of any number of hits depending on what elements the page includes.

The number of unique users *does* provide useful information. For example, an increase in the number of unique users demonstrates that your marketing efforts are proving successful. What you really need to know is the success of each individual marketing activity, allowing you to focus on the successful ones. This can be achieved in two ways.

One option is to create a *landing page* designed to follow up on each marketing campaign. For example, if you run a TV ad, you can have a webpage at http://www.yourDomain.com/TV that supports the commercial, letting users make the transition from ad to site. Extra work is required to build the landing page, but after it's built you can track users arriving at that page and be confident they have come via a certain campaign.

The alternative is to *tag* your links with additional information. Instead of linking to http://www.yourDomain.com/index.html, you link to http://www.yourDomain.com/index.html?campaign=tv. Your website will ignore anything after the question mark, but the whole address will be recorded in your website stats. This means you can track any users with campaign=tv and know they came from that particular campaign.

This approach requires no additional pages, but the addresses aren't user friendly. This doesn't matter online because people are clicking links, not typing addresses; but you should avoid this technique for offline promotions.

This technique has become so popular that it's supported by many stats packages including Google Analytics. When it's set up, Google can tell you much more than how many visitors a campaign generates. It can also provide information about leads and conversion rates.

Monitoring conversions

Most website have a call to action they want users to complete, such as signing up for a newsletter, completing a "contact us" form, or buying a product. Whatever the goal, you need to track how many users have completed it and which marketing campaign generates the most responses.

A *lead* is a person who completes a call to action. But your *conversion ratio* is a more interesting figure: it compares the number of people who arrive at your site and those who complete the call to action.

Google Analytics provides a URL builder to help format web addresses in a way that lets you tracking marketing campaigns.

This helps when you're comparing individual campaigns. For example, Google Adwords generates a higher conversion ratio than viral marketing, because those who respond to viral marketing don't have an existing need. Those clicking on a search advertisement do.

Track the conversion ratios of campaigns to establish which offer the best return on investment. But your site can also affect conversion ratios. If a site is hard to use, fewer visitors will complete a call to action. That brings us to the next role of statistics.

Finding and resolving problems

If your conversion rate is low across all marketing initiatives, it could reflect a problem with your site. This could be due to any of the following:

> *Usability*—The user is unable to find the call to action due to poor navigation or other usability issues.

> *Browser compatibility*—For example, a particular browser may not render the site correctly and so users can't complete the call to action.

> *Content*—The site doesn't provide adequately convincing content to encourage users to complete the call to action.

What constitutes a low conversion ratio depends on your call to action. An e-commerce site may have a ratio anywhere between 0.5% and 8% depending on the sector and product. On the other hand, a call to action that doesn't cost the user money should yield a higher ratio. The best approach is to compare a conversion ratio against itself over time. As you make adjustments to your site, do they harm or improve the conversion rate?

Website statistics can also suggest what changes will improve your conversion rate. Start by looking at where users exit your site.

Dropout points

Immediately exclude those who view only one page, or the home page will be at the top of your list. This is because people click through from a search engine, discover this isn't the site they want, and leave immediately. Now, look at the remaining pages. Why are users leaving at these points? Is the content relevant and clearly presented? Is the navigation usable? Are you suggesting a next step to the user, or are these dead-end pages?

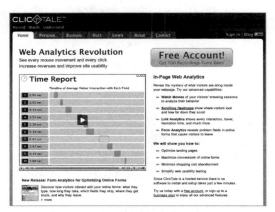

ClickTale (http://clicktale.com) lets you anonymously record users interacting with your website.

Look at the history of users who drop out at a particular page. How long have they been on the site at this point? What other pages have they viewed? How long did they spend on the exit page before leaving? Does this reveal trends that help to identify the problem?

Sometimes the problem is obvious; other times it isn't. In such cases, try usability testing. This will uncover potential issues. If usability testing isn't an option, try using a tool like ClickTale (http://clicktale.com).

ClickTale picks up where traditional analytical packages leave off. It records user sessions anonymously, showing you what users click or hover over and how far down the page they scroll. Although a technology like ClickTale is impressive, it can't replace traditional usability testing. It doesn't provide the opportunity to question the user. For example, it can't explain why users abandon shopping carts.

If you're the owner of an e-commerce site, you may be horrified by the dropout rate on shopping-cart pages and think you have a fundamental usability problem. But in many cases, that isn't true. Questioning users reveals that they abandon baskets for a host of reasons ranging from "I was saving the items to buy later" to "I wanted to compare the price on another site." Shopping carts always have a high exit rate, and no amount of statistical analysis can change that.

But statistical analysis can help you improve the content and products you provide on your site.

Identifying popular content

There is an obvious benefit to understanding what users want from your site. From what content they're looking for to what products they will buy, understanding users' requirements lets you mold the site to meet their needs.

Website statistics can help identify popular content, but not in the way you may expect. Looking at the most-visited pages won't provide answers. Popular pages can be misleading for three reasons:

> Pages can be visited by mistake.

> Pages can be popular because they're prominent.

> Pages can be popular because they're gateway pages to deeper content.

Users don't always behave logically or predictably. In some situations, statistics don't reveal their motivation.

The home page is a good example of these problems. I have already explained that it's visited by mistake from search engines. It's also a prominent page and used as a navigational tool for finding other content.

Looking at how long users spend on a page helps to weed out false positives, but it can give you only a partial indication of the popular content on your site. A better approach is to look at the search terms users enter into search engines to reach your site. Almost all website analytical packages provide this information, and it helps define users' priorities. But this only gives you information about content that already exists on your site. If a user entered a search term for content you don't have, your site wouldn't have been returned. The user would never have come to your site. What you need is a way to identify content that you don't offer but that users want.

If you fail to use the same terminology as your users, they will be unable to find your content and will go away frustrated.

You can do this by examining the phrases users enter into your *own site's* search engine. As I wrote in chapter 8, "Taking control," approximately half of your visitors will use internal search. Every time they use search, they're telling you exactly what they want from your site in their own words. That data is incredibly valuable. You need access to these search terms, particularly the ones that return zero results. Users are expressing an interest in a piece of information you don't have or your search engine doesn't recognize.

When you have access to these search phrases, start tailoring content around them. If the content doesn't exist, add it where appropriate. If it does exist but isn't being found, introduce the exact phrasing your users are searching for.

Analyzing your web stats can provide a valuable insight into your site and how users interact with it. But don't let working with web stats replace meeting and testing your site with real users.

Next actions

Your website is a part of a broader marketing strategy. You can't launch a website and sit back while visitors pour in. Equally, you can't rely on search engines alone. You need to utilize existing offline marketing material to promote your site and engage with users wherever they are online.

If your fledgling website is going to be a success, you need to take action now:

ACTION 1: *Start tracking.* Ensure that you can track the stats on your site. Unless you already have a stats package, install Google Analytics. It's free and only requires copying and pasting some code into your site.

ACTION 2: *Get listed.* Ensure that your site appears in search-engines results. Start by adding yourself to Google (http://www.google.com/addurl) and other search engines like Yahoo! and MSN. Do this right away, because your site can take several weeks to appear. In the meantime, consider using Google Adwords. It will get you instantly listed, and you have complete control over the cost. Adwords campaigns also appear in Google Analytics, so you can easily track the success of these campaigns.

ACTION 3: *Target your audience.* Identify one or two community sites where your target audience congregates, and begin to participate. At the same time, approach as many blogs and magazine sites as are appropriate to your audience. Offer to write about a subject of interest to them.

This should be more than enough to attract a new audience and ample to keep you occupied now that the site's build stage is finished.

After you've attracted your new visitors, you need to keep them engaged. They're unlikely to complete your call to action on their first visit, so you must attract them back again. That is the subject of the next chapter.

11

Engaging
your visitors

In this chapter

When most organizations launch their first website, it's nothing more than an online brochure. Customers don't have the opportunity to respond in a meaningful way or communicate with one another. This model was born out of years of mass marketing.

But the web is changing, and you need to alter the way you communicate with your users. The web is becoming an ever more community-focused medium. High-profile sites such as YouTube, Wikipedia, and Facebook are built around communication between those running the site and individual members.

This community spirit is also spilling over into the commercial sector as organizations such as Dell and Microsoft recognize the benefits of transforming their users from a mass of individuals into a living community. These companies have seen the power of community revitalize damaged brands, improve products, and even reduce costs, but it has come at a cost.

Many marketers struggle with the idea of open two-way communication with customers. It's a model in which the message can't be controlled and is sometimes unpredictable. Why then should you make your site more than brochureware? What are the benefits of cultivating a community?

THE POWER OF COMMUNITY

For many, the Holy Grail of a successful website is *stickiness*. How do you keep users coming back for more?

Repeat users are incredibly important. These are the people who develop brand loyalty, complete calls to action, and regularly purchase. According to data from Web-SideStory Inc. (http://bit.ly/4AbgXq), repeat users are eight times more likely to make a purchase on an e-commerce site. Such users are the lifeblood of most websites.

One of the best ways to keep users coming back is to foster a community. A thriving community provides many benefits in addition to repeat traffic. An online community can also

> Improve your offering

> Change brand perception

> Promote your site

> Reduce your costs

Let's examine how.

Google Analytics lets you track how many repeat visitors your site attracts.

Improving your offering

A good community isn't just about users speaking to one another through a forum or chat room. It's also a two-way dialogue between you and your users. It's an opportunity for you to hear from your users and discover what they want from your website.

In an attempt to refine their products or hone their marketing message, many organizations spend substantial figures on focus groups and customer surveys. But a healthy community is constantly providing feedback about your offering. This gives you superior insight into how your product or service should develop, at little or no cost.

Listening to your users also improves their perception of you.

Changing brand perception

People like to be heard. They like to feel that their opinion matters. Engaging with your users and *really* listening to what they have to say about your products and services is incredibly powerful. It's even more powerful when they see their suggestions acted on.

A lone blogger (Jeff Jarvis) created a ground-swell of negative opinion about Dell after frustrations with the company's customer service. Dell acted to engage with the community and went (in the words of *Business Week*) from "worst to first."

By talking to customers and engaging the community around their products, both Dell and Microsoft have significantly improved the way their brands are perceived. Often, such an effort involves nothing more than a speedy response to a complaint and an apologetic tone. Openness and transparency with a community can also go a long way.

It's possible to both undo a negative brand perception and nurture a positive one. When users feel positive about your brand, they will recommend it to others.

Promoting your site

A community that is enthusiastic about your site or products can be one of the most powerful promotional tools available. Sites like Digg have become popular largely because of their passionate community. Equally, Apple's success is at least partly due to its obsessional fans, who promote Apple products with friends and family. Nothing is as valuable as personal recommendations.

If you include your users in the process of developing your site, they feel invested in it. They feel the site is as much theirs as yours and so will promote it as their own. A successful community is always seeking to draw others in, thus growing and promoting your site. This evangelistic tendency in a community can also lead to substantial cost savings.

Reducing your costs

A passionate community can provide free advertising and save you money on focus groups and product development. It can also reduce your customer support costs. This is particularly true if your site already provides customer support. Rather than send queries directly to you, users can post them in support forums; others in the community can then answer the questions. These forums also become a repository of knowledge

iPod touch

Product	iPod touch
Recommendation:	Neutral - Mid product cycle
Last Release	September 09, 2008
Days Since Update	80 (Avg = 185)

Recent Rumors

Recent Releases
???
9/2008
2/2008

11/17: Apple to Introduce an iPod Stick?
11/16: iPod Nano 1.0.3 Update Adds In-Ear Headphone Support
11/13: IBM's Lawsuit Against Papermaster Over 'Racetrack' Memory? [Update]
11/12: Apple Positioning iPhone and iPod Touch as Mobile Gaming Devices
11/04: Apple to Benefit Further from Dropping Flash Memory Pricing
...more...

iPod nano

The iPod nano is Apple's midrange iPod; it was previously known as the iPod mini

Product	iPod nano
Recommendation:	Buy - Product recently updated
Last Release	September 09, 2008
Days Since Update	80 (Avg = 285)

Recent Rumors

Recent Releases
???
9/2008
9/2007
9/2006
2/2006
9/2005
2/2005

11/17: Apple to Introduce an iPod Stick?
11/16: iPod Nano 1.0.3 Update Adds In-Ear Headphone Support
11/13: IBM's Lawsuit Against Papermaster Over 'Racetrack' Memory? [Update]
11/12: Apple Positioning iPhone and iPod Touch as Mobile Gaming Devices
11/04: Apple to Benefit Further from Dropping Flash Memory Pricing
...more...

iPod shuffle

Product	iPod shuffle
Recommendation:	Buy - Product recently updated
Last Release	September 09, 2008
Days Since Update	80 (Avg = 223)

that others can draw on. This reduces the support burden (and cost) for your organization.

Finally, communities have a lower cost of sale. People who are already enthusiastic contributors to your community are easier to reach. This is especially true for repeat ordering. How do you build a successful community? A big part of that process is choosing the right tool.

> Apple recognizes the reduced costs of selling to existing customers, which is why the company constantly updates its product line. There is even a site dedicated to tracking these updates (buyersguide.macrumors.com).

THE RIGHT TOOL FOR THE JOB

Community is about more than technology. Too often, website owners think that if they add a forum or blog to their site, they will have a community. Adding the technology is easy. Nurturing and growing that community is the challenge.

But tools do help shape the community. Different tools fulfill different roles. If you use the wrong tool, no amount of nurturing will make the community grow. It's therefore important that you understand the tools available. You can use three types of community tools:

> Broadcast tools

> Feedback tools

> Interactive tools

Let's look at how each works.

Using broadcast tools

Broadcast tools let you communicate with your community but don't allow your community to respond. They generate interest but don't nurture community.

Some organizations use these tools because they're fashionable, without understanding their role. It's important to be aware of each tool's strengths and weaknesses as well as the job they perform. These tools include the following:

> *Blogs*—Most organizations fail to grasp the potential of blogging. Many corporate blog posts are merely press releases and do nothing to nurture community. An effective blog should build personal relationships with users. It should be personal and engaging and encourage feedback via comments (see "Using feedback tools").

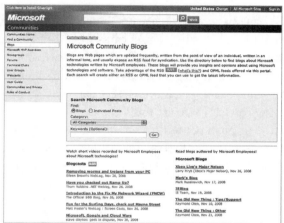

Microsoft has improved its image by encouraging individual employees to blog about their work. This openness has helped humanize the company and improve customer relationships.

> *Podcasting*—Podcasting can be more time consuming than blogging. It also has search engine optimization and accessibility issues. But it's still a powerful way to engage with visitors. As with radio or television, consumers feel they know the presenter and experience a personal connection. Most successful podcasts have a substantial number of passionate followers who naturally form a community. Podcasts are also less common than blogs, so it's easier to stand out from the crowd. Finally, podcasts can be accessed away from the PC via MP3 players. This allows users to listen during their commute or at the gym, and attracts an audience other broadcast methods may not reach.

Gary Vaynerchuk produces a daily wine podcast (http://winelibrarytv.com/) that receives 100,000 downloads per episode and promotes his wine retail business. Gary attributes the success of the show to his community.

> *Email newsletters*—Organizations have been sending email newsletters for years. Because of their proliferation and the growth of spam, they're becoming less effective as a broadcast tool. They're often ignored or, worse, deleted by spam filters. That said, they should be part of your strategy for encouraging repeat traffic— they have a proven track record for bringing people back to your site.

Web feeds (also known as RSS) have begun to replace email newsletters. They're also an integral part of both blogging and podcasting. Users can subscribe to a web feed of a blog, a podcast, or another information source. This feed is then delivered to a feed aggregator. Such aggregators are integrated into all kinds of software including Microsoft Outlook, Internet Explorer, and web applications. Users can thus see updates from numerous sources without having to visit each site individually.

Web feeds are an excellent way to push content to interested parties without relying on them to checking your website regularly. The downside of web feeds and all the tools mentioned so far is that they focus on pushing content to users. To create a community, you need to hear from users.

Using feedback tools

As we have already established, the power of community lies in hearing from users. Feedback tools make this possible. Feedback comes through a variety of mechanisms, but I'll focus on two: email and surveys.

Email feedback

When a user clicks a contact link or completes a feedback form, eventually the resulting message ends up in somebody's email inbox. What happens then is crucial to the way users perceive your website and organization.

Take time to consider how you'll handle email feedback. Who will respond to the emails? How will you track your conversations with users? How will you prevent emails from falling between the cracks?

Responding to email in a timely manner is important especially when it comes to making users feel appreciated. Be sure you have a process in place and individuals who are responsible for ensuring that email is answered.

Don't let user inquiries get lost in the system. Every email needs to be responded to quickly and efficiently.

The drawback with email is that although the feedback is valuable, it's hard to analyze. Sometimes you require something more structured.

Surveys and questionnaires

Many websites use surveys and questionnaires as a way of gathering feedback that can then be analyzed. There is no shortage of companies offering to add a questionnaire or survey to your site. Yet surveys and questionnaires are harder to implement than you may expect. Although the technology is simple, getting quality feedback is difficult. Some ways to improve the effectiveness of a survey include the following:

> *Keep it short.* As I said in chapter 2, "Stress-free planning," the longer your survey, the less likely a user will complete it. Focus on gathering specific information.

> *Show appreciation.* Recognize that users' time is valuable. If a user completes your survey, offer them a reward, or at the very least say thank you.

> *Keep it simple.* Avoid questions that require too much mental effort. Start with easy questions (such as the user's name) and build up to more challenging ones.

> *Be specific.* Asking questions that are open to interpretation can lead to unhelpful feedback. For example, asking "What do you think of the site?" may lead to comments about security when you want design feedback. Providing context for a question or using an example can bring clarity.

> *Avoid noncommittal answers.* If you ask people to rate something from 1 to 5, many will answer 3. Such noncommittal answers provide little value.

> *Watch your language.* Wording can substantially affect results. For example, using the word *should* instead of *could* can alter results by up to 20%.

Be careful how you interpret results. Users are unlikely to complete a survey unless they either like or hate your site, leading to polarized results that need careful interpretation.

Email, surveys, and questionnaires aren't the only tools for gathering user feedback.

Uservoice (http://uservoice.com/) is part of a new generation of customer feedback tools. More open ended than a survey or questionnaire, it lets users request new features and vote for others' suggestions.

Interactive tools are even better suited to building a community and encouraging multiple-way communication.

Using interactive tools

Combining broadcast and feedback tools helps create a dialogue with your users, but doing so doesn't build a true community. That requires a dialogue between users. When users start communicating with each other, you gain the benefit of repeat visitors and community interaction.

Community isn't limited to your site. In the last U.S. election, Barack Obama engaged with his community of supporters via the social-networking tool Twitter.

Many interactive tools can help build community. The right tool depends on the size and maturity of your community. For example, launching a chat room doesn't mean a community will appear, because a chat room requires a critical mass of users before it's effective. If this critical mass doesn't exist, users will find the chat room empty and won't return.

The following table shows various interactive community tools and explains when it's appropriate to implement them.

Interactive community tool (community size)	Description
Ratings (small/large)	Allowing users to rate pages, products, or other elements of your site is a good way to begin building your community. It requires little effort from users and yet provides real value to others. It also provides valuable information for the website owner.
Mailing list (small/medium)	Mailing lists are a great way to get users talking to one another and to you. They're ideal for small communities because all users see every message. But be warned: mailing lists don't scale well, and a large number of messages from a bigger community can become annoying.

Interactive community tool (community size)	Description
Reviews (medium/large)	Writing a review requires more mental effort than rating a product from 1 to 5. As a result, fewer users complete them, and a bigger community is required. On the other hand, they provide more value to the community and create better communication between users.
Comments (medium/large)	The ability to comment on articles, blog posts, and other content is extremely popular. Like reviews, comments require a degree of effort on the part of users. They also require more people to maintain a sufficient level of activity.
Forums (medium/large)	Forums are the most popular community tool, but they only work effectively for medium to large communities. Often, forums lie dormant if they don't have sufficient users to remain active. Nobody wants to be the only person at the party!
User-generated content (large)	Many high-profile communities such as YouTube, Facebook, and Wikipedia rely on their users for content. Relying on and allowing users to create content is the ultimate expression of community. It requires a large number of dedicated users to be successful.
Chat room (large)	You need a large community of visitors regularly visiting your site to support a real-time chat room. If you don't have such a community, a chat room can lie empty most of the time. Users will stop coming because they presume the community is dead.

Before building a new community, ask yourself whether there are existing communities you could use. There is little point in re-creating a successful community like Facebook. That said, if you decide to start a community, begin with ratings and slowly progress through the interactive tools until you have enough committed users to support forums and eventually a chat room. Of course, having the right tools is only a part of the battle. It's important to know how to communicate with users successfully.

SUCCESSFUL COMMUNICATION

It's important to set the right tone for your community through the way you communicate with your users. Successful communication is trickier than it first appears. It depends on two factors:

> When you communicate

> How you communicate

Get this wrong, and you risk seriously damaging your relationship with users.

Knowing when to communicate

Your communication schedule is always important, whether you're posting to a blog or sending out a newsletter. Send too many communications, and they become irritating; send too few, and users forget about you.

This frequency depends on the nature of your site. If your site sends out stock tips, then users may expect updates every few minutes. If you sell a service that is purchased once every couple of years, then sending out communications every few weeks will be enough.

The key is regularity rather than frequency. Users should come to expect your communications. Communicating on an ad-hoc basis becomes frustrating for users, especially with blog posts, newsletters, and podcasts.

Internet media company Revision3 (http://revision3.com/) recognizes the importance of regular release dates, which is why it has set broadcast times for all of its shows.

But communication doesn't have to be entirely dictated by a schedule. You can also have trigger-based communications. These are normally emails sent to a specific individual rather than the entire community. They're sent in response to a specific event rather than a schedule.

Common trigger-based communications are the emails sent to users who have just purchased from an e-commerce site. These typically include one email confirming the transaction and one when the goods are dispatched. Such emails are extremely important but are often overlooked in the development process.

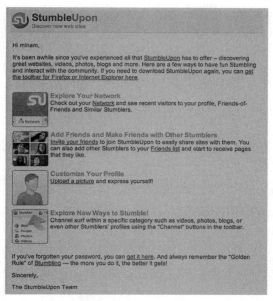

Stumbleupon.com tries to tempt lapsed users back by reminding them of the site's key features.

Trigger-based communication also encourages repeat traffic. Most website communities have a large number of *sleepers*. These are individuals who have signed up for the site but have stopped using it. It's possible to monitor user activity; if a user stops using your service, you can automatically send an email that tempts them back with incentives or new content.

Never forget the golden rule of user communication: don't contact users without their permission. Nothing will damage your site's reputation and destroy your community more quickly than spam.

Take a few moments to consider your communication strategy. When might it be appropriate to send out trigger emails? Are you collecting users' contact details, and is it legitimate to contact them? What methods do you use to communicate, and on what schedule? Your communication with users needs the same attention you give your site's copy. This includes not only when to communicate, but how.

Understanding how to communicate

We've already talked about the mechanisms for communication such as blogs, podcasts, email, and RSS; but these are just technologies and don't get to the heart of how to communicate. Communication is about what you say and how you say it.

Always remember: when you're communicating with users, make it personal. Whether you're responding in a forum or posting to your blog, people like to talk to other people, not faceless corporations. Whenever possible, write as "Jim from Marketing" rather than as "Acme Inc." Users are less critical and more receptive when they're dealing with an individual rather than an organization.

Although your aim is to demonstrate that your organization is made up of real people, you still need a unifying voice.

Know your voice

The danger of individual employees engaging with your users is that your organization may send mixed messages about its identity. All copy should have a consistent tone, from the content on your website to the emails you send existing customers.

This may seem contradictory. On one hand, I demand that you have a consistent identity; and on the other hand, I want users to see the people behind your organization. Newspapers have been employing this approach for years.

Most newspapers have recognizable columnists. But each newspaper also has an overall identity. For example, in the U.K., the tabloid newspaper *The Sun* has a very different persona than *The Times*.

Deciding on your persona will underpin all your communications with users. Ask yourself this question: if your site was a person, what type of person would it be? Would it be a young, hip teenager, or a boring, middle-aged business man? These characteristics help define how you communicate and the tone you set for your site. Whatever persona you create should always be open and transparent.

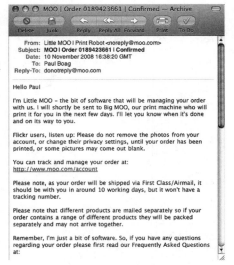

All emails from print company MOO (http://moo.com) are written as if sent by a piece of software called Little MOO. This persona is somewhat gimmicky but strangely appealing.

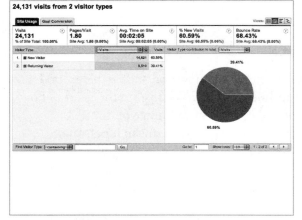

Photo-sharing site Flickr (http://www.flickr.com) is always quick to acknowledge when it makes mistakes.

Be open and honest

Many organizations feel they need to maintain a flawless facade with users. This serves to create a barrier, reinforcing the feeling that the user is dealing with a faceless corporation.

A better approach is to be honest and fallible. Nothing is more effective in getting users' trust than admitting when you're wrong. Take the photo-sharing site Flickr. The site suffered a series of outages in which users were unable to access their photos. Unsurprisingly, the mood in the Flickr community was negative. But Flickr was able to turn that negativity around with a simple blog post entitled "Sometimes We Suck." The company acknowledged the problem, apologized, and promised to do better. It then did exactly that—and before long, Flickr was seen as a shining example of how an organization should run a community.

It *is* possible to turn a critical user into an evangelist for your site by responding to them in a timely and open manner. Users can instantly broadcast their frustrations via blogs, social networks, and other methods of online communication, so you can't afford to ignore them. But if you respond in a positive and open fashion, those same users will broadcast their pleasure at your response.

Of course, to respond to a user in a timely and open manner, you first need to encourage that user to communicate with you by fostering a sense of community.

FOSTER A COMMUNITY

The sad truth is that most website owners only hear from users when there is a problem. "I can't get this to work!" "Where is this piece of content?" "Why don't you offer this feature?" Although it's possible to nurture community out of such negative correspondence, it isn't community in itself. There is no sense of loyalty to your site and certainly no interaction between users.

How do you move from superficial interactions to something that provides the benefits of community?

Most website owners only hear from users when they have a problem.

Controlling growth

Creating and running a community is like gardening. You must seed and nurture it, especially in the early days when it's vulnerable. As it grows, the amount of work is reduced and you reap the harvest. But care is still required, and you may need to prune to stop your garden from growing in unwanted directions.

Setting aside the analogy, let's look at some practical ways you can grow your community in a controlled manner.

Surviving the early days

The early days are the toughest and require a lot of work. Get things wrong, and the community will be stunted and may die. Fortunately, the following five techniques will increase your chances of success:

> *Start small.* Many website owners are too ambitious when creating a community. As I explained earlier, some community tools need a large community to support them. But it isn't just about the type of tool—it's also about the way you set it up. Take forums, for example. Start with only a couple of categories, to concentrate your users in one place. If they're spread across multiple categories, they're less likely to connect. It's like a party, where it's better to have all your guests packed into a small house than rattling around in a large empty hall. By keeping people together, you help generate buzz.

Nothing is more awkward than being the first at a party. The same is true with an online community. Make sure your guests are packed together so they experience some buzz and interaction.

> *Seed the discussion.* It falls to you as the host of your community to encourage conversation. You can do this by seeding discussion. Ask open-ended questions, request feedback, and show a genuine interest in what people have to say. Too many bloggers complain that nobody comments on their blogs, but they never ask people their opinion.

> *Nurture the conversation.* When users begin engaging, you need to maintain the momentum. Conversation can easily run dry if you don't nurture it. Respond quickly to comments with follow-up questions. Even if you disagree with a comment, thank the user for their input and encourage more posts. Don't disagree directly. Instead, ask whether they have thought about your alternate view and what their opinion is. This encourages more conversation and avoids belittling them. Responding to comments is time-consuming in the early days, but it's required for successful growth. Responding is worthless if users are unaware of your response, so always ensure that users can be notified of responses by email or RSS.

> *Set boundaries.* All communities require rules to maintain healthy discussion. Having a set of guidelines for acceptable behavior is important, but it isn't enough. A community is defined by its leadership, and users learn the way to behave from the example you set. If you're cheeky and irreverent, then they will respond in kind.

Leadership by example is particularly important when you're resolving conflicts. Whether the conflict is between two community members or involves you, never respond aggressively—doing so will only escalate the conflict. Responding in a considered and calm fashion encourages others to do likewise. Finally, never respond to conflict in an open forum. Deal with it discreetly via email, to limit fallout.

> *Avoid unnecessary moderation.* Many organizations hesitate to introduce a community for fear of what users may do or say. They're torn between the benefits of a community and the fear of not being able to control that community. This leads to excessive moderation, where contributions are checked before release.

Some organizations worry about the legal ramifications if a user posts something inappropriate. Others fear negative comments about their organization. Both fears are unjustified. Although you have legal responsibilities, the risk is minimal if you respond to complaints by removing the offending content. And negative comments can increase the credibility of your site. They prove you don't edit user contributions and thus reinforce the authenticity of positive comments. If the number of negative comments outweighs the positive, then your community has helped identify a problem that needs fixing. By fixing the problem, you demonstrate that you care about your users.

Both of these perceived risks are less damaging than unnecessarily censoring user comments. Censorship stunts community growth by slowing communication and generating mistrust in your audience. User contributions should be removed as a last resort.

If you follow these guidelines, your community has every chance of growing. But sustaining that growth in the long term is challenging.

If users feel as though you've bound and gagged them, they won't contribute to your community.

Demand-based growth

As your community grows, the risks begin to change. The emphasis shifts to maintaining growth. The biggest temptation is to grow too quickly.

A handful of users may request a forum, and you create one. Others ask for more categories in the forum, so you add them. The problem is that a handful of users isn't always enough. You should experience a significant demand for new features before you implement them. Without that demand, new features won't be used, and your community will appear to be dying. It's the party analogy I gave early: better to have users concentrated in one or two community features than spread thinly across several.

Knowing when to expand is difficult. Do it too early, and you give the impression that your community is unpopular. Do it too late, and you frustrate users because their ideas aren't being implemented. No matter how hard you try, you'll make mistakes.

Don't be afraid to remove features that aren't working. Pruning is an essential part of a successful community. It's especially important for older communities, where numbers are beginning to decline. If you don't have enough people to support a

The Boagworld forum (http://boagworld.com/forum/) relies heavily on community leaders to encourage new members, stimulate discussions, and police community rules.

forum, be willing to move to a mailing list, which is better suited to smaller numbers. You'll find that doing so stimulates new growth.

A growing community also brings scaling problems. When a community becomes large, it's difficult to follow everything. It's hard to nurture new members, and the community feels like a full-time job. Although the benefits of community are high, they don't normally justify that level of commitment.

The solution is to utilize your community. As the community grows, enthusiastic members will emerge—regular contributors who are full of suggestions and ideas about how the site could be improved. Ask these people if they want to be community leaders and effectively help run the community. Their role will be to moderate content, resolve disagreements, and encourage conversation.

In my experience, such users normally agree and volunteer their time for free. They see it as an acknowledgment of their commitment and a chance to help shape the community. It also tends to deepen their commitment to the community, turning them into evangelists. It makes them feel important—which is one reason people participate in communities to begin with.

Feeding the community

It's easy to focus on the benefits a community can bring to your organization and fail to consider what it offers users. Why will they participate? Unless you can provide an incentive, they won't bother to participate, and your community will never grow.

When I use the word *incentive,* your mind may turn to some form of financial incentive. This is one way of encouraging users to participate. Competitions, vouchers, discounts, and prizes do help draw people in. But they don't build long-term loyalty and, if handled badly, can create problems.

Netscape's attempt to buy users' loyalty ultimately failed, and the site was closed.

For example, Netscape offered $1,000 per month to top users on Digg if they posted to Netscape instead of Digg. Although this action generated a lot of press, it backfired and reflected negatively on the Netscape brand. The site ultimately closed.

Fortunately, the motivation behind participating in a community is more subtle and less expensive than material incentives. Much of it is sociological. Users are motivated to participate because of four basic desires:

> *The desire to associate*—We are social creatures. We desire to associate with like-minded people and those we admire This is a major motivator, and you need to ensure that it's met. Welcoming new members is important because it makes them feel valued. Encourage their contributions, and listen to what they say. Most important, build a community persona whom people want to associate with.

You may be fortunate enough to have a strong brand like Apple that people like to associate with. In most cases, you won't. Fortunately, communications full of personality can take your brand a long way. This is perfectly demonstrated by Innocent. Innocent sells fruit drinks, which don't naturally generate a strong sense of community. Nevertheless, the company built a vibrant community through passionate personality and some clever little ideas.

> *The desire to impress*—We all want five minutes of fame, and the web make that possible. Online communities in particular offer an opportunity to stand out from the crowd. Many users contribute to communities to demonstrate their knowledge or have their say. Although this egotistical motivation can be problematic, it's a powerful driver in getting people to contribute, and you should encourage it.

As I mentioned earlier, asking people to become community leaders is one way, but there are others. Allowing users to vote on content submitted by others can be a motivational tool; it encourages users to post quality content. Providing users with titles or badges if they post often also encourages quantity.

> *The desire to reciprocate*—A lesser motivation is the desire to give back to a community that has helped the user. If users have received help and support from a community, they sometimes feel motivated to offer the same to others. You should encourage this feeling. Ensure an outstanding first experience in the community by responding quickly to contributions and making users feel welcome.

> *The desire to express*—Many people are initially drawn to a community because they have a strong opinion they wish to express. They're either happy or displeased with their experience of your site/company, and they want to make

Innocent smoothies (http://www.innocentdrinks.co.uk/) has a vibrant community that is actively involved in the development of the product. This "family" even raised money for charity by hand-knitting 500,000 wooly hats to go on the bottles. With some creative thinking and a friendly persona, any brand can build an active community.

those feeling known. If you want to make users into regular contributors, it's important to do two things. First, ensure that their comments aren't moderated or edited. If users feel censored, they will go away angry and frustrated. Second, respond to comments quickly; and no matter how unjustified, recognize their feelings. Make them feel you've taken their comments on board.

By responding to these needs, you'll encourage participation. With this plus controlled growth, your community will flourish.

Next actions

Community is a powerful business tool. It's a great way to retain customers, promote your site, improve your product, and reduce your costs. In this chapter, we've explored the tools of community and the techniques for launching and maintaining that community.

Understanding the principles of creating an effective community and putting them into practice are two different things. It can feel like an overwhelming task, but you can begin the process in three simple steps:

ACTION 1: *Establish the potential.* Before you begin to invest in community tools, establish whether there is a need. Do you receive regular requests for community features? At the least, you need a large newsletter subscriber base to work with. If you have neither, consider adding a survey to your site to see if users are interested. If nobody completes the survey, then they're unlikely to contribute to a community. If they do and are positive, then there is potential.

ACTION 2: *Gather the resources.* After you've established potential, you need to secure resources. A community needs a leader who is committed to checking the site regularly and responding to user contributions. It's a big job, so it's important to find somebody who has the time and people skills to carry it out. You also need to implement the tools of community. Remember to start small—for example, with ratings and comments. Finally, you need to establish an "approach" to the community. These are guidelines about how the community is run and operated; they cover issues such as dispute resolution and moderation.

ACTION 3: *Commit to the long term.* Realize that building a community is a long-term commitment. It won't happen overnight. You need buy-in from your organization if the community is going to survive. The return on your investment will take time to materialize.

Building a community isn't your only long-term commitment. The site and your entire web strategy are long-term commitments. You should always be looking to the future and thinking about the next step. That is the topic of this book's final chapter.

12

Planning for the future

In this chapter

B efore becoming a web designer, I trained in print design. Although I enjoyed it, I always hated the finality. After something was sent to press, there was no turning back.

The web doesn't have these constraints. You can launch a site on Monday and tweak the design or content on Tuesday. This is both a blessing and a curse.

It's a curse because it feels as though the work will never end (and it won't). It's a blessing because your site can dynamically change and adapt with your business and user requirements.

It's your job as website owner to shape this evolution.

How do you plan the future of your site? How do you ensure that it's flexible enough to adapt to the rapidly evolving web? What are the emerging trends, and where do you look when you're keeping an eye on the future?

The key to planning for the future is accepting that most of us have the wrong attitude toward web design.

A BROKEN MODEL

Most organizations have a throw-away mentality that works like this: A company commissions a rebuild of its website. The new site is launched, and everybody is excited. As time goes by, the site begins to age. Content goes out of date. The design doesn't reflect changes in brand or audience. Technology becomes obsolete. Eventually, the website is seen as an embarrassment.

Everyone in the company knows the site is a problem, but nobody is responsible for solving it. Finally, a member of senior management decides the site must be prioritized, and a new version is commissioned. The old site is thrown out, and the cycle begins again. This process is wasteful for two reasons:

> *It wastes money.* Completely replacing the old site every two to three years is a waste of money. You replicate work that was already done, rather than build on what exists.

> *It wastes potential.* The website spends much of its life unused because those in your organization are ashamed of it. Your site should be working hard to generate leads, support customers, and fulfill other functions throughout its entire life cycle.

This situation damages the way your organization perceives the web. Instead of seeing it as a powerful tool that supports your business, it's seen as a significant expense.

If your site is left untended, it will become out of date. Eventually, it will be viewed as a liability.

Users visiting your site midway between redesigns see something out of date that doesn't reflect your organization.

For your website to have a long-term future, you need to stop periodic redesigns and embrace continual development. This is a significant cultural shift, especially from a financial perspective. Most organizations perceive their website as a periodic capital expenditure (like buying a new photocopier) rather than an ongoing investment (like their marketing budget). This needs to change.

In chapter 3, "The perfect team," I explained the benefits of phased development. Those same benefits apply here. Continual development provides a financial benefit for these reasons:

> *Work isn't thrown away.* Instead of replacing previous development work, you enhance it.

> *Cash flow improves.* You replace a major capital investment every few years with a smaller ongoing commitment.

The redesign model is partly born out of the way organizations engage with their web-design agency. This relationship also needs to change.

Periodically redesigning your website almost always results in the previous website being discarded. This is a wasteful approach.

A BROKEN RELATIONSHIP

Unless they have an in-house web team, most organizations don't regularly speak to their web designers. Instead, they hire an agency on a per-project basis. Many believe it's good practice to change supplier every couple of years. It isn't.

Whatever the case, the website owner normally defines the project, writes the brief, and sets the scope. Although this approach is appropriate when commissioning an agency for the first time (or when replacing an incumbent), it isn't ideal. It's flawed for three reasons:

> *It's time consuming.* Finding, choosing, and briefing agencies takes time. Taking on these new agencies also perpetuates the redesign cycle, because each agency wants to stamp its own mark on the site.

> *There is a learning curve.* The new agency has a steep learning curve before it understands your business enough to deliver an

It's important to have an ongoing relationship with the team that built your website.

effective solution. Even an incumbent agency has a learning curve. Things may have changed dramatically in the months (or years!) since the agency last worked on your site.

> *The agency's role is stifled.* Web designers should be more than implementors. Traditionally, the website owner defines the brief, and the agency responds. But this arrangement provides no opportunity for the agency to contribute ideas to the site. The site fails to benefit from the agency's expertise.

If the future lies in the continual evolution of your site, then you must break down the barriers between client and agency. You and your team need to *really* engage in order to move your site forward.

A good web-design agency should constantly suggest new ideas to you. It should share what it has learned from other projects and from the industry at large. You can then decide which of these ideas apply to your business.

Web designers aren't just experts in building sites; they're also experts at the web. They're aware of what other sites are doing and what is possible. Use this knowledge.

This kind of relationship takes time to develop. The agency needs to understand your business and objectives before it can make suggestions. This won't work if you regularly change suppliers or talk to your agency only every couple of years.

Arrange regular meetings with your agency. Encourage it to share what it's been doing on other projects and what innovations it has seen online. Invite suggestions.

You may think that having an in-house team will foster this relationship. After all, an in-house team will know the business and always be around to make suggestions.

Having in-house capacity offers many benefits (see chapter 3), but it also has some drawbacks. An in-house team doesn't work on other websites and so can't learn from those sites. Many in-house teams are preoccupied with day-to-day maintenance rather than long-term strategy.

Whether you have an in-house team or use an external agency, make sure they report trends they see emerging online. These trends are the future of your web strategy.

If you use an external web designer, ask them to share ideas from other projects. You may find some of them are applicable to your site.

TARGET EMERGING TRENDS

I started designing websites in 1994, and back then it would have been impossible to imagine the web of today. It's foolish to predict the long-term future of your website. Things move too fast. But it's possible to see the next big thing.

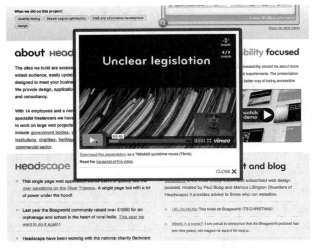

The combination of video-hosting sites like Vimeo (http://www.vimeo.com/) and the spread of broadband means that an increasing number of sites are introducing video content.

I could write on entire book about emerging trends, but I believe these three trends are relevant in the short term:

> The growing prevalence of rich media

> The rise of the API and widget

> Web strategies that look beyond the website

You should decide which of these trends are applicable to your site in consultation with your web-design team. Each involves emerging technologies more complex than the other topics found in this book. I'll outline what is possible, but you'll need further advice if you're interested in implementing these ideas.

Creating a richer experience

Audio and video have been on the web for years. Recently, the widespread adoption of broadband and improved compression techniques have increased their prevalence.

From YouTube to iTunes, audio and video have become intrinsic parts of the web—and yet many website owners haven't integrated them into their web strategies. Some of the possibilities for using rich media include the following:

> *Starting a podcast*—In chapter 11, "Engaging your visitors," I explained the benefits of podcasting. Many people believe it's too complicated for them to use. In reality, podcasting can be done on a shoestring budget with basic equipment. People are attracted to a podcast not for its production values but because of the content and presentation. But although podcasting can be done on a shoestring budget, it requires a long-term commitment to be successful.

> *Using video demonstrations*—Often, the best way to demonstrate your product or website is to show it to people. Whether it's a video of your product, a panoramic overview of a venue, or a screencast about using your site, video can communicate a lot of information in a short time.

> *Adding video testimonials to your site*—Customer testimonials are an excellent way to convince potential converts. Traditionally, these have been written, but video testimonials are more engaging and convincing than their text equivalents.

> *Engaging with users through video streaming*—With only a webcam and a computer, you can speak directly to your users through services like Ustream (http://www.ustream.tv/). Doing so provides a unique opportunity to build community and engage with users via text, video, and audio.

> *Publishing to sites like YouTube*—In chapter 10, "Driving traffic," I talked about using YouTube as a viral marketing tool and the challenges associated with doing so. You can also use YouTube as a communication tool to reach existing customers, a method for publishing video podcasts, or a hosting platform. It was once hard to add video to your site. Now, sites like YouTube make it easy.

YouTube isn't the only service that lets you easily add functionality and content to your site. You have many opportunities to leverage the hard work of others to improve your own site.

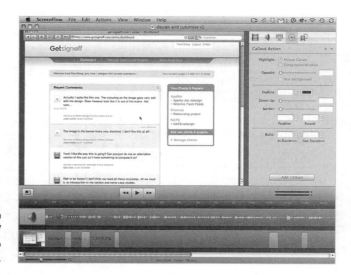

Screen-capture tools like ScreenFlow (http://www.telestream.net/screen-flow/overview.htm) make it easy to develop video tutorials that introduce users to your site.

Standing on the shoulders of giants

Isaac Newton said, "If I have seen further than others, it is by standing upon the shoulders of giants." As a website owner, you have the opportunity to do the same.

Many people offer services and content that can integrate for free with your site. What would cost a fortune to implement from the ground up becomes considerably more straightforward. These web services fall into three broad categories:

> *Web feeds*—RSS is by far the most prevalent way of integrating third-party content into your site. This is because it's easy to create RSS feeds. An enormous number of sites provide RSS feeds you can use. Feeds are available for weather, news, events, photographs, music, and much more. Some coding is required, but it isn't complex; and third-party websites like Feed Informer (http://feed.informer.com/) can help with the process. Many sites let you upload content and use RSS to display that content on your own site. For example, instead of developing a costly event-management system, you can use Upcoming (http://upcoming.yahoo.com/) and its RSS feed to add events to your site.

> *Widgets*—Widgets are small pieces of code that, when added to your site, provide additional functionality. Adding a widget only involves copying and pasting. Literally thousands of widgets are available, even though they're more complex to develop than RSS. Unlike RSS, widgets do more than display content; they also allow interaction. You can use widgets to display interactive maps, order products, run surveys, post notifications, and much more. Although widgets are powerful, it's often hard to customize their appearance and almost impossible to change the way they work. For that, you need an API.

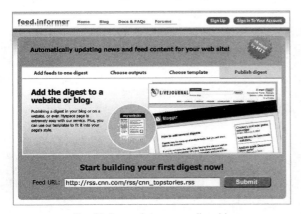

Feed Informer lets you easily add
an RSS feed to your website.

Widgetbox (http://www.widgetbox.com/) has
thousands of widgets that you can add to your website.

> *APIs*—An API is the most powerful method for integrating third-party functionality. It's a set of tools that a web developer can use to interact with a web application at the code level. APIs are both powerful and flexible when compared to other options. It's possible to send data to and receive it from third-party sites as well as manipulate and present that data in a large variety of ways. APIs are often used to provide the same functionality as widgets but in a much more customizable way.

These web services let you create functionality more quickly than building from the ground up. You can also combine multiple web services to create even more sophisticated applications called *mash-ups*. For example, Twittervision (http://beta.twittervision.com/) takes posts from social-networking site Twitter and displays them on a map using the Google API.

The danger of web services is that your site becomes reliant on their functionality. If the site providing the web service goes down, then your own site may also experience problems. It's therefore important to be confident in the uptime of the service before you integrate it. This isn't often a problem with services provided by companies such as Google or Yahoo! But you may wish to be more careful with smaller sites. The best approach is to ensure that the site is still usable even when these services fail.

That said, web services can save you a lot of time in development, and they allow functionality that may normally be beyond your budget. The challenge is to keep up with the growing number of services being released. You may reinvent the wheel because you don't know what is available. That is why you need an ongoing dialogue with your web-design team.

Web services can also reach those who never even visit your site.

Looking beyond your website

Websites are a passive way of engaging potential customers. They rely on users coming to the site and initiating contact. Relying on this as the sole means of online engagement is a failure to utilize the potential of the web.

It isn't your website that matters but your *content*. For example, let's say you run a conference and have a website that encourages people to attend. What matters more: that people see your site or that they attend your conference? The answer, of course, is the latter.

Chapter 10 talked about engaging users through emerging social networks such as YouTube, Facebook, and Twitter. But these are techniques you should be implementing *now*! As you look ahead, you need to plan ways not only to take the conversation to your users but also to deliver your content to them.

Building web services

The secret to distributing content is to use web services. Whereas previously I encouraged you to use those produced by others, now I suggest you create your own.

RSS, widgets, and APIs are all excellent ways to reach a wider audience. They do this by releasing content from the constraints of your site.

As you plan for the future, consider how these technologies can spread your message. Do you have content or functionality that other website owners may want?

For example, Amazon provides tools that let website owners add products to their sites. These range from commission-earning links to full embedded shopping catalogues. Amazon recognizes that these services reach a wider audience than that of its website.

Whether users see your website is irrelevant as long as your web strategy achieves its desired aim.

Amazon lets website owners earn revenue by adding widgets to their sites. The company recognizes that widgets can reach a larger audience.

This approach isn't limited to selling products. Everyone from news organizations to TV channels are beginning to push content beyond their websites.

Some web services are more difficult to build than others. Adding an RSS feed that sites can use to syndicate your content is straightforward. Implementing an API is more challenging. Creating a basic widget can often be a good middle ground. Although building a widget takes time, it's easy to add to a site, which encourages adoption.

Depending on your audience, you should consider building applications for social networks like Facebook or MySpace. These sites provide frameworks that let third parties build applications. Users can then add these applications to their profiles. Building applications can be time consuming; but if your audience uses these sites regularly, it may be worth the effort.

In the future, web services and applications won't be the only way to extend the reach of your website.

Computer-friendly content

Tim Berners-Lee (the creator of the world-wide web) has been working toward the next evolution of the web: the semantic web.

The semantic web will enable computers to understand web pages much as people do. They will be able to complete many of the tasks that consume our time online. For example, they will be able to find content more efficiently than we can, using services like Google.

The semantic web doesn't need to be part of your short-term plans. The technologies involved are still evolving and are some way from being mainstream. Nevertheless, you can take some small steps now, like building your site using *microformats*.

Microformats provide a standardized ways of marking up content in HTML, allowing computers to better understand what that content is about. For example, if the information about a conference was marked up using microformats, then it would be possible for a computer program to extract that information and display it on another site.

MapQuest (http://www.mapquest.com/) uses microformats to display longitude and latitude as well as events.

Although microformats have yet to be widely adopted, they're still worth implementing. It's easy for your developer to build a site using microformats, so there is no reason not to do so. As more sites use microformats, more applications will emerge that use them. Eventually, your content will become compatible with other sites at little cost to you.

So far, I have focused on distributing content to other sites. But it's also possible to distribute content to other platforms.

TARGET EMERGING PLATFORMS

Traditionally, the web has been accessed using a browser on a computer. But websites are beginning to appear on the desktop and also on a variety of devices from cell phones to game consoles. It's important to consider whether you should include these emerging platforms in your web strategy. How do you make that decision?

Looking beyond the PC

It's astounding how many devices can now access the internet. Cell phones, game consoles, watches, personal organizers, even refrigerators can all display web pages.

Some of these gadgets can be ignored as too niche or as passing fads. But others, like the cell phone, are much more significant, as I explained in chapter 7 ("Ensuring access for all"). With mobile devices accounting for 19% of web usage, it's an emerging market that you should monitor.

Unfortunately, building your site using the best practices described in chapter 7 isn't enough to ensure that it's effective on these alternative devices. The same website that serves desktop users won't necessarily help those with alternative devices, due to two factors:

> The environment

> The device

Let's look at how these issues effect developing for these platforms.

Samsung has released a refrigerator with an integrated touch screen, allowing users to watch television and access the web.

The importance of environment

The majority of websites are designed for users sitting in front of a computer. This is a relatively controlled and predictable environment. Users are normally indoors, can use both hands, and tend to give the computer most of their attention. But that isn't always true for other devices.

The environment can vary depending on whether you're walking down the street looking up directions on your cell phone or relaxing on the couch watching YouTube on TV. These environmental (or contextual) differences affect the design and content of your site.

Take, for example, a user accessing your site on a cell phone. They're likely to be out and about, with the associated noise and distractions. This

Someone accessing your site from a cell phone while standing at a bus stop has a different experience than a PC user. Your site needs to accommodate these differences.

environment demands both a simplified design and clearer, more concise content. Users won't read large amounts of copy via a mobile device. The type of content they require is also different. A user accessing a mobile device is much more likely to want information such as addresses or contact numbers, and less likely to want access to product demonstrations or visually intense information.

Accessing the web on a TV introduces still other environmental factors. Unlike a computer, users view a TV from a significant distance and interact with it using a remote.

Opera has worked with Nintendo to produce a web browser for the Wii. This lets users surf the internet from the comfort of their armchairs.

Most TVs also have a lower resolution than the average computer monitor. These factors combine to have a significant effect on the design of your site.

Before you decide to support a device, consider how the user's environment will alter your site's design and content. You may conclude that the content you provide on your existing site isn't appropriate. You may even decide that supporting these devices is pointless because the situation or audience is wrong for your offering.

If you see potential in designing a site for cell phones or other devices, also consider their limitations.

The limitations of the device

Alternative devices differ from PCs in technology as well as context. Cell phones, game consoles, and other devices all have significant differences that affect the user experience. These include the following:

> *The rendering engine*—Not all devices display web pages as well as a PC does. Cell phones in particular have trouble displaying HTML pages correctly. In addition, many devices struggle with audio, video, and other media. These problems are diminishing as devices become more sophisticated.

> *The screen*—Devices come with an enormous variety of screens. Some are monochrome, others have low resolution, and most come in nonstandard sizes. A website that displays perfectly on most PCs will require horizontal scrolling on a TV and be unusable on a cell phone. Fortunately, CSS can help, but this requires additional coding.

> *Input methods*—Whereas most PC users have a mouse and keyboard, those using other devices may use any number of input methods: remote controls, motion sensors, touch screens, numeric keypads, and so on. This has a huge impact on how the user interface is built. Once again, CSS can provide the answer by presenting different designs optimized for each device.

> *Connection speeds*—Increasingly, sites developed with PCs in mind rely on broadband connections. They're graphically intensive and use audio and video. But some devices have less robust connections to the internet. Cell phones in particular have poor connectivity, especially in rural areas. Sites designed for these devices need to be streamlined as compared to their PC counterparts.

Catering to alternative devices isn't straightforward, but an increasing amount of web traffic will come from these devices. Cell phones need to be a part of your long-term strategy.

In the short term, focus on preparation. Build your site with the latest web standards, which can be easily adapted for emerging devices. Also think about what content the users of these devices will want and in what environments those users will be using such devices.

Amidst all this planning for alternative devices, don't forget the desktop.

Moving to the desktop

A new breed of desktop application is emerging that is built using web technologies. These applications

An iPhone may be able to access traditional websites, but the smaller screen, slower speeds, and touch interface change the experience.

> Are easier to build

> Don't require software developers rather than web designers

> Can reuse many of the technologies already developed for your website

Although there are a number of different ways to create web-powered desktop applications, the most common is to use Adobe AIR (http://www.adobe.com/products/air/). AIR lets you build applications that run on all the major operating systems using HTML, CSS, JavaScript, and Flash.

This opens up some exciting possibilities. But just because you can do something doesn't mean you should! Before you incorporate a desktop application into your web

eBay has built a desktop application using Adobe AIR that lets users monitor their bids.

strategy, consider whether it's appropriate. Do you need a desktop application, or will a traditional website suffice? Ask yourself the following questions:

> *Do your users have intermittent connectivity?* Those using desktop applications are unaffected if they have no connection to your site. This is ideal for users with dial-up connections or who are traveling. But do your users *need* access to your content while offline? In most cases, they're happy to wait until they're connected again.

> *Are users entering a lot of data?* If you need users to complete long online forms, then you may want to consider a desktop application. Such applications tend to be more reliable and less likely to lose data in transit to your web server. Nothing is more annoying than losing work because your connection times out.

> *Do users require fast access?* Even AJAX-driven websites don't respond as quickly as desktop applications. Users who are continually using a portion of your site (such as a contact directory) may become frustrated by poor performance. In some situations, a fast response is required for other reasons. For example, a customer-service representative requires a fast response when looking up answers for a customer who is on hold.

> *Do you need to integrate with the operating system?* Certain situations may require you to integrate more closely with the operating system than a normal website allows. For example, you may want to add a system-tray notification that informs users when a certain event happens on your site (like a new article being published). Alternatively, you may wish to have a more sophisticated file-upload facility than that provided by the browser.

If your website is primarily content driven, then you probably don't need a desktop application. But if your site is a heavily used web application, it may be worth considering.

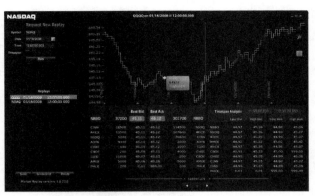

Information available through the NASDAQ site is also available to traders in a constantly updating desktop application.

AIR applications are ideal for intranets, social networking, and any site that requires regular notifications to be sent (such as a stock ticker). But in most cases, they're unnecessary.

There are many more innovations that you could include in your web strategy. The challenge is to be aware of what is possible.

STAY INFORMED

This book has taught you the essentials of running a successful website, but I can only start you on the journey. I've provided a strong foundation; now, in order to harness the power of the web, you need to stay informed.

This can seem like an overwhelming prospect, but it doesn't need to be. It's a matter of soaking in information from as many sources as possible. Much of it will be irrelevant to your circumstances, but occasionally you'll learn about something that will take your site in a new direction.

How do you find those nuggets of inspiration when you have limited time? Here are some tips that will help:

> *Get an RSS reader.* If you don't subscribe to RSS feeds, then you should start. Get an RSS reader, and subscribe to a number of web-design blogs. I particularly recommend Gerry McGovern (http://gerrymcgovern.com/new_thinking.htm) and A List Apart (http://www.alistapart.com). For a round-up of web-design-related stories, subscribe to my feed at http://boagworld.com/feed/. After you subscribe, scan the headlines each morning, and see if anything jumps out. This shouldn't take more than 10 minutes a day.

> *Subscribe to a web-design magazine.* Magazines can provide an overview of emerging innovations. They also have the advantage that you can read them while away from the PC. I recommend that you start with *.net magazine* (http://www.netmag.co.uk).

> *Attend local networking events.* Speaking to other site owners and designers is both inspiring and educational. Regular local meetings are held all over the world, so you should be able to find one in your area. A good place to start is your local chamber of commerce or an events site like Upcoming (http://upcoming. yahoo.com/). Upcoming allows you to search on web design in your area.

Subscribe to a web-design magazine like *.net.*

> *Listen to a web-design podcast.* You can listen to podcasts while commuting or at the gym. Doing so avoids cutting into valuable time but keeps you informed about the web. Unsurprisingly, I recommend my own podcast, which is available at http://boagworld.com.

For further advice on running a website and a newsfeed about latest innovations, visit my blog and podcast at http:// boagworld.com.

> ➤ *Get involved in a forum or mailing list.* Join an online community of website owners or web designers. A variety of forums and mailing lists are full of people facing similar challenges and willing to share advice. You may wish to consider the Boagworld forum (http://boagworld.com/forum) or those at SitePoint (http://www.sitepoint.com/forums).

> ➤ *Read just one book.* I don't want to overwhelm you with an extensive reading list, but I would like to recommend Steve Krug's book *Don't Make Me Think!* (New Riders Press, 2005). Usability is one of the most important aspects of running a website. Although I covered the basics in chapter 6, "User-centric design," this is such an important subject that further reading is recommended.

> ➤ *Go to at least one conference each year.* Conferences are an excellent way to spot emerging trends and hear some of the most talented people in the web-design world. Attending one a year will probably be enough to keep you informed. Unless you're fortunate enough to work in a sector that has its own web-design conference, I recommend one of the "Future of" conferences run by Carsonified (http://events.carsonified.com).

Running a website is challenging, and it's hard to do in isolation. Wherever possible, engage with others doing the same job, and learn from their experiences.

Next actions

And so we reach the end of this book, but not the end of your journey. My underlying message has been the ongoing nature of your website and your role as website owner.

This chapter in particular has focused on the need to look forward. We've looked at emerging trends and platforms. And, most important, we've examined your relationship with your development team. Get that right, and you stand a much greater chance of success.

What now? Well, you could put this book aside and get on with your work. But let me suggest three final things you can do instead:

ACTION 1: *Look at your site with fresh eyes.* With all you've learned from this book buzzing around your brain, now is a good time to take a fresh look at your site. Put down your preconceptions and history. Allow yourself the freedom to dream.

ACTION 2: *Arrange a meeting with your team.* Don't limit brainstorming to yourself. Arrange a meeting with your design team, and encourage them to share their ideas for the site. Don't worry about things like budget and time scales; try to picture what your perfect website would look like. You can worry about practicalities later.

ACTION 3: *Visit Boagworld.* Finally, I encourage you to visit my website at http://boagworld.com. In addition to the podcast and newsfeed I've already mentioned, the site contains hundreds of posts and articles about every aspect of running a website. If there is an issue I haven't written about, email me, and I'll try to cover it.

Let me conclude with some words of encouragement. Running a website can seem like a daunting task, but it's also incredibly exciting. The web is a medium where you can easily correct your mistakes—and that gives you amazing freedom. It's the new frontier of marketing, business development, and business strategy. The web is a wonder of human achievement, and you get the chance to contribute to it. Enjoy the opportunity.

INDEX